D1705352

RENÉ GUÉNON
AND THE FUTURE OF THE WEST

THE LIFE AND WRITINGS OF A 20TH-CENTURY METAPHYSICIAN

ROBIN WATERFIELD

RENÉ GUÉNON

AND THE FUTURE OF THE WEST

THE LIFE AND WRITINGS
OF A 20TH-CENTURY
METAPHYSICIAN

SOPHIA PERENNIS

HILLSDALE NY

Second edition 2002
First edition, Crucible Books 1987

© Sophia Perennis
All rights reserved

No part of this book may be reproduced or transmitted,
in any form or by any means, without permission

For information, address:
Sophia Perennis, P.O. Box 611
Hillsdale NY 125295
sophiaperennis.com

Library of Congress Cataloging-in-Publication Data

Waterfield, Robin E. (Robin Everard), 1914–2002
René Guénon and the future of the West : the life and writings of a
20th-century metaphysician / Robin Waterfield.—2nd ed.

p. cm.

Includes bibliographical references and index.
ISBN 0 900588 87X (pbk: alk. paper)
ISBN 1 59731 019 0 (cloth: alk. paper)
1. Guénon, René. 2. Philosophers—France—Biography. I. Title.
B 2430.G84 W38 2002
194—dc21   2002000071

TO DR MAX WARREN
Canon of Westminster Abbey
in piam memoriam
and
TO MY WIFE SOPHIE
in eternal regard

ROBIN WATERFIELD

spent his early years in the Sudan and France. After rejecting a medical career in favor of publishing, he studied Jung and became a member of the Jung Institute, as well as running a home for maladjusted children with his wife. He spent sixteen years in Iran working with the Persian Episcopal Church and for many years ran a bookshop in Oxford. He passed away just months before this book was reprinted.

ACKNOWLEDGMENTS

My thanks are due to the All Saints Sisters for housing us, to Ellic Howe and to Martin Murphy for advice and practical assistance. Dr H.G. Ostwald has helped by sharing his profound knowledge of the *Tao* and the *I Ching* and by many stimulating conversations which helped me to clarify my ideas about the Primordial Tradition. Robert Appleby has been a patient listener and sounding board for some far-out ideas. Lester Kanefsky's valuable comments came, alas, too late to be made full use of but were nonetheless valuable. Mrs Tamsin Dunningham has proved a fast and reliable converter of my difficult manuscript into readable form. To all—my heartfelt thanks.

REW

All men will come to him
who keeps to the one,
for there lie rest
and happiness
and peace

The Tao

CONTENTS

Acknowledgements ix
Introduction 1

Part One

1. Early Days 11
2. Searching 19
3. Finding 28
4. Cutting the Ties 32
5. Breaking Loose 38
6. Turning to Mecca 43

Part Two

Introduction:
The Wounded Amazon 50

1. Clearing the Ground:
Reason and Beyond 56
2. Crossing the Mediterranean:
The Encounter of East and West 67
3. The Voice Behind the Fan:
Tradition and Society 78
4. The Spiral Staircase:
Cosmic Cycles and the Reign of Quantity 86

5 The Primal Vision:
  Symbols and Truth 101
6 In Search of the Lost Word:
  Initiation and Spiritual Growth 113
7 A Priest Forever After the Order of Melchizedek:
  The Moment of Vision 125
8 Christ and Cosmos:
  The Rabbi of Nazareth and His Teaching 133
  Select Bibliography 140
  Index 147

INTRODUCTION

SOME THIRTY YEARS AGO Thomas Merton succinctly de-scribed the situation that confronts us all:

> The world of our time is in confusion. It is reaching the peak of the greatest crisis in history. Never before has there been such a total upheaval of the human race. Tremendous forces are at work, spiritual, sociological, economic and not least of all political. Mankind stands on the brink of a new barbarism, yet at the same time there remain possibilities for an unexpected and almost unbelievable solution, the creation of a new world and a new civilization the like of which has never been seen. We are face to face either with Antichrist or the Millennium, no one knows which.[1]

Since then the struggle seems to have gained in intensity, the dividing lines have become clearer, the process of disintegration—or, as Guénon called it, dissolution—has proceeded at an ever-increasing rate. People's hearts are truly failing them for fear as all their familiar landmarks are being swept away and they can discern no firm agreed basis for any course of action. Our brief hopes that science and 'the experts' would usher in the new millennium have been rapidly dashed; all we have left now is a plethora of 'experts' contradicting one another.

This sense of confusion and fragmentation had its origin a long way back in Western history. Guénon has often been accused of being uninterested in history as the West understands it and even of being anti-historical. It is certainly true that the minutiae of the history of the West did not interest him very much, though he never denied them a certain relative importance. But since he was steeped

---

1. *The Silent Life* (1957), p173.

in the vast panoramic vision of the East, he saw the whole process of what we call the Christian era as being only part of a period in the great cosmic cycle known to the Hindus as a *Manvantara*.

The whole duration of the manifest creation or phenomenal world is called by the Hindus *Kalpa*, and is believed to consist of fourteen *Manvantara*s, each *Manvantara* having a duration of 64,800 years. The Christian revelation deals only with the present *Manvantara*, now reaching its end.

With this perspective in mind it is easy to see how, for Guénon, the last 2,000 years could be seen to be relatively unimportant. Nevertheless, Guénon by no means ignored it, but found within it certain turning points marking the end of a smaller cycle within the larger one. One such date was that of the suppression of the Knights Templar by Pope Clement V at the Council of Vienna in 1312 and the subsequent torture and execution of the last Grand Master of the Order, Jacques de Molay, in 1314. Other focal points would have been the Renaissance and the rise of Luther and Protestantism, the Age of Enlightenment and the Industrial Revolution.

Guénon believed that from the beginning of the nineteenth century onwards the pace accelerated and the speed at which things decayed quickened very noticeably. It is unlikely that he knew much about William Blake, but if he did he would certainly have endorsed Blake's lines in his prophetic poem *Jerusalem*, published in 1808:

> They left the Sons of Urizen the plow and harrow, the loom
> The hammer and chisel and the rule and compasses...
> And all the Arts of Life they changed into the arts of death in Albion
> The hourglass contemned because its simple workmanship
> Was like the workmanship of the plowman and the water-wheel
> That raises water into cisterns, broken and burnt with fire
> Because its workmanship was like the workmanship of the shepherd:
> And in their stead intricate wheels invented, wheel without wheel
> To perplex youth in their outgoings and to bind to labors
> In sorrowful drudgery to obtain a scanty pittance of bread in Albion...
> In ignorance to view a small portion and think it All
> And call it Demonstration, blind to all the simple rules of Life.

Later on in the century the painters, dazzled by recent scientific theories, invented *pointillisme,* which foreshadowed Guénon's 'reign of quantity'. In such paintings the smooth surface presented by reality to our normal sight was fragmented into a series of tiny colored dots, which the viewer by an effort to induce an optical illusion had then to restore to the smooth surface of normal vision. This manifestation of the quantitative as opposed to the qualitative aspects of reality was the subject of Guénon's last major work, *The Reign of Quantity and Signs of the Times* (1945). In the field of the visual arts the multiplication of images by means of photography is one example. The influx of artistic influences from all over the world from countries with traditions and cultures very different from our own overwhelmed the European tradition in all the arts and fragmented it so that no one firm tradition remained in which an artist could mature and with which he could experiment. Many have commented on the subsequent dehumanization of art, notably the Spanish philosopher Ortega y Gasset, who remarked on the separation of art and craft and the rise of art for art's sake and its increasing privatization until it became the preserve of a selected few instead of the pleasure of many. This general process of dehumanization was movingly expressed in the life and work of the greatest painter of our age, Pablo Picasso, who in his vast painting of the bombing of Guernica foreshadowed the fragmentation of the world by war, which we can now anticipate in all its finality in the real possibility that one day all may be dissolved into a vast cloud of atomic dust.

In music and architecture a similar dehumanization can be seen. Corbusier's notion of houses as 'machines for living' is one example. Skyscrapers and tower blocks, which ignore human scale and for purely economic reasons cram the greatest number of living units onto the smallest possible ground space regardless of human welfare, are another. Atonal and electronic music present equally pertinent variations on the same theme. Examples from literature, from James Joyce and *Finnegan's Wake* to the work of William Burroughs and his arbitrary and aleatory methods of composition, demonstrate that fragmentation and dehumanization can be seen in every form of artistic endeavor. The Surrealists sought the absolute in the absurd, while Sartre claimed in *La Nausée* that the contingent was the ultimate reality. The average man tries desperately to find some firm foothold in the cosmic storm raging around him. The ways of escape from the reality of our situation are legion, but none help us to face the reality.

Very early on, probably even before the First World War, René Guénon realized that Western civilization was doomed to ever-increasing decay and dissolution; his life was devoted to enunciating the immutable principles on which alone mankind can rely with absolute certainty, and which could help us through our situation.

Like all great teachers his approach is essentially supra-personal. The facts of his life, the sources of his knowledge, the historical and personal factors which encouraged him to write and say what he did, are of interest, particularly to the modern Western mind, which is obsessed with the personal. But ultimately they are irrelevant. What matters most is the message he transmitted. As Nadjmoud-Dine Bammate says:

> For René Guénon truth alone is what convinces by its own intellectual evidence. There is no place for the persuasive power of an individual or the dialectical skill of an author. Nothing should cloud the clear mirror of what is. The thought, not Guénon's thought, but the thought which is transmitted by him, does not require authors, scarcely even interpreters. It is made known by a process of transmission which is both exact and rigorous. It is thus that it affirms its truly traditional character. Guénon did not claim to be a thinker but a messenger.

It is this impersonality and authority that many find so baffling and even repellent in Guénon's writings. Some have noted an aggressive element in some of his work. It is certainly true that such an element exists and that much of his writing is in the form of critiques of other people's work, whose errors he relentlessly exposes. But in his best and most important works this element is largely missing. But the impersonality and the authority remain. Both of these qualities are curiously disconcerting and are, I believe, related to one another. In most writing in the West today the personality of the author is all too painfully evident. His 'personal slant', as we call it, enables us to agree or disagree with him on personal grounds and to justify our attitude by a variety of intel-lectual tricks. These tricks include what may be called psychological reductionism on the lines of: 'Considering his childhood and his relations with his parents, we can easily explain why he thought as he did'; or a more general relativization that considers a writer predominantly in his historical and cultural setting and as the product of a continuing stream of ideas that will inevitably be superseded by fresh thoughts and newer ideas and can therefore be disagreed with. Such judgements are made on the basis of a strong presumption that what is new is better than what is old—an evolutionary theory that Guénon constantly rebutted.

We shall never grasp Guénon's message if we approach it in these ways, for he frequently states that he is *vox et praeterea nihil,* consistently and rigorously excluding the personal, subjective ele-ment from his writing. He maintained a strict privacy and refused all attempts to disrupt it, and he resisted equally all attempts to make him adopt the role of *guru,* or a Master, or a wise man of any kind, seeking disciples and followers.

How then are we to approach him and his message? Firstly, surely, by concentration on the content of the message and not on the character of the messenger; an attitude of mind which, if we can achieve it, brings with it a great sense of freedom and openness. Secondly, readers will be helped if they accept the fact that Guénon's message is not the dry statement of a set of intellectual propositions, to which we can assent or not as we wish, but a challenge to a new way of life, which if accepted will affect every aspect of our thinking and acting. The truths that Guénon enunciated can only be understood by being lived, *crede ut intellegas;* they are what the French call *verité vécue*—lived truth. It should also be borne in mind that his message is coherent, every aspect of it supporting and clarifying every other, and so cannot be understood or accepted piecemeal.

All this may sound to our frail and confused minds as smacking of brainwashing or of autocratic authoritarianism. Nothing could be further from the truth. As I have said, Guénon's writings do not provide a rigid, all-embracing system into which we have somehow to cram ourselves, accepting it all passively without contributing our own personal understanding or experience. Guénon believed that living by the Tao meant rejecting all notions of systematization:

> The highest good is like water.
> Water gives life to ten thousand things and does not strive,
> It flows in places men reject and so is like the Tao.

This adaptability and fluidity Guénon believed was characteristic of what he called the Primordial Tradition, which can be equated with the Tao.

We may say, then, that the message of the Primordial Tradition is rather a series of guidelines or pointers to help us find our way through the all-enveloping fog in which the Western mind now wanders. It also furnishes us with a series of danger signals, alerting us to the subtle and damaging traps with which the path is strewn.

It is indicative of the state of the West that Guénon's work has been largely ignored. Even in his native country it can still be said to be the concern of only a few. Perhaps this will always be the case for its rigorous and fundamental rejection of all the modern sacred cows, shibboleths, and of the terms of reference governing modern thought, can never command wide acceptance. As P.M. Sigaud, the editor of a large collective work on Guénon, remarks:

> He demands of the reader a profound conversion to his way of thinking, for he sets out intrepidly to reveal the universal and eternal metaphysical principles which are the antithesis of contemporary relativism.

Once these principles have been grasped, everyone is free to apply them in his or her own way and to feel secure because the underlying principles of action and living are universal and immutable.

The role of Guénon was thus to proclaim principial truths rather than to show how they should be applied, since their application is a personal matter. The writings about Guénon since his death have demonstrated the very wide range of interpretations and applications of which his work is capable, from the sociology of work in Jean Hani's *Les Métiers de Dieu* to the nature of Surrealist thought in Eddy Batache's *Surréalisme et Tradition*. Philosophers have discussed his restoration of metaphysics; Freemasons have underlined his importance as a restorer of authentic Masonry; Christian theologians have debated whether he is for or against their beliefs. One such, Henri Stéphane, has said that he thinks that every Christian, tired of feeble apologetics for the faith, should immerse himself in Guénon's works and would emerge a better Christian for having done so.[2]

One sad but inevitable consequence of the interest in Guénon in France is that his thought has become reified and rendered largely sterile by those who wish to see it as something static, to be used as an infallible textbook giving the correct attitude to be adopted when confronted with a problem or situation. People refer to *l'oeuvre guénonienne* and are described as *guénonians*, all of which I am sure Guénon himself would have deeply deplored had he been alive to see it, and which he vigorously opposed when he saw signs of it in his lifetime.

Because there is always the danger that one may misinterpret Guénon's thought, his books will always generate discussion. I have not seen fit myself to neglect entirely the biographical approach to him, nor to remain unaware of the particular psychological characteristics that may have contributed to the way he enunciated his understanding of the Primordial Tradition. Some of his followers, as disciples always will, have been tempted to impute omniscience and infallibility to him; I cannot follow them. For me, as for Guénon, or so I believe, we all have to respond in our own individual way, taking into account our own personal circumstances, making our encounter with Guénon a lived truth, by applying the principles he enunciated to our own particular situation. In the words of the old Anglican collect, we should 'read, mark, learn and inwardly digest' his work.

Guénon, for all his apparent dogmatism, was a modest man. Like Milarepa he did not really want adoring disciples; he much preferred to have friends. Some 3,000 years ago the *Tao Te Ching* described the qualities of the sage as resembling those of a pregnant woman:

> Opening and closing the gates of heaven
> Can you play the role of woman?

---

2. *Introduction à l'Ésotérisme chrétien*, vol. 2, pp 58–59.

> Understanding and being open to all things,
> Are you able to do nothing?
> Giving birth and nourishing,
> Bearing and yet not possessing,
> Working yet not taking credit,
> Leading yet not dominating,
> This is the Primal Virtue.

Guénon possessed this Primal Virtue in good measure. I hope this book does not betray the friendship I feel for him and that it may help others to feel a like friendship.

PART ONE

René Guénon in 1908

1

EARLY DAYS

Few lives are less susceptible to dramatization or investigative journalism than that of René-Jean-Marie-Joseph Guénon, born on November 15, 1886 of parents no longer young. His father, Jean-Baptiste, was 56 and his mother 36 at the time of René's birth. Jean-Baptiste came from a family of small landowners, whose prop-erty consisted mainly of vineyards and who can be traced back to a Jean Guénon born in Saumur in 1741. In the course of time René's grandparents moved to Breze, a nearby wine-growing area, where his father was born, the elder of two sons. The wives too were members of similar families in the locality. What is evident is that Guénon was entirely French in his ancestry and, what is more, French without an admixture of Celtic or Mediterranean stock. Coming from the heartlands of France gave Guénon a strong sense of being rooted and of belonging to a given place and a given culture which, as it has been for many Frenchmen, was an almost mystical source of confidence for him.

Jean-Baptiste Guénon did not wish to spend his life managing the family vineyards, so leaving this to his younger brother he proceeded to study architecture. By the time René was born the family was living in Blois in a small house in the rue Croix-Boisée in the suburb of Vienne on the left bank of the Loire, where his father was carrying on his employment as an architectural expert.

Shortly before René's birth his parents had lost a much-loved baby daughter, Jeanne, who died only two months before René was born. One can imagine the joy with which his arrival was greeted and the intensely protective care with which he was surrounded. As it turned out this was necessary, since from birth the young boy suffered ill-health. He was so fragile that he was given an emergency baptism at home and only formally baptized in church some time after. The family was deeply religious and an atmosphere of piety was pervasive, although their piety did not prevent them from making some efforts to contact their dead daughter through a spiritualist medium.

When René was seven his father became a loss-adjuster for a large local Assurance Society and the family moved from their little house in the rue Croix-Boisée to a bigger house with a garden in the faubourg du Foix on the Quai du Foix facing the river.

This was the house where the formative years of Guénon's childhood were spent and to which he returned in later life as a haven of safety in the bosom of his family. Since he was always delicate he did not go straight away to school. Instead his primary education was undertaken by his mother's sister, a widow named Madame Veuve Duru who lived next door to them, and who was herself a schoolteacher.

At the age of eleven he was confirmed in the parish church of St Nicholas in Blois and made his first communion. So René grew up in an atmosphere of bourgeois piety, the spoilt darling of his aunt, who had no children of her own and lavished all her affection on the delicate little boy placed in her care. His mother, though no doubt much loved, seems to have played a smaller part in his life than her sister the widow. His elderly father may have been a source of René's subsequent interest in mathematics, and may also have allowed his son to know something of his work of drawing up plans and surveying, but of this there is no documentary evidence.

This period of comfortable sheltered bourgeois life quite naturally gave way to greater contacts with the outside world when at the age of eleven René was sent to begin his formal education in the secondary school of Nôtre Dame des Aydes, a school with a religious foundation staffed by secular priests, the syllabus being identical with that of a minor seminary. The school was well-established in old buildings in the rue Françiade in the highest part of the town. The headmaster at the time was a certain Canon Orain, the staff were sympathetic and well-qualified, and the classes were small.

Guénon joined the school in the autumn of 1898 as he was nearing his twelfth birthday. He proved to be an exceptionally talented pupil and soon mastered the syllabus, very often coming first or second in his class. It is interesting to note that the subjects in which he did not do so well were drawing, literature and French compositions, the latter were judged by his teacher, the Abbé Bossard, to be too short and incomplete. Clearly, imagination and an artistic sense were not a prominent part of René's make-up. His conduct, appearance and application were all rated as very good.

His undoubted scholastic success was achieved in spite of frequent illnesses and consequent time off school. This brilliant student was soon seen to be a loner, and though well thought of by his contemporaries left curiously little impression on them when they looked back in later years. Even his closest friend only recalls the long silent walks they took together to and from school. There is no doubt that he suffered from certain psychological weaknesses, which he never entirely outgrew.

These came to light in an incident of seeming triviality which nevertheless proved to be of considerable importance for René's future. It seems that during the autumn of 1901 Guénon was not happy with the treatment he received from his teachers. He seems to have believed that one of them at least 'had it in for him'. René's father wrote a letter to the headmaster accusing one of the teachers, M. Simon Davancourt:

> Yesterday evening for more than an hour in the school and even in the street [he] created a scene which made him ill and René was compelled to retire to his bed with a serious fever. We fear complications and are very disturbed.

This was written on October 19 and on October 22, before he had received an explanation from the headmaster, René s father wrote again to the head in terms which will surely now seem to be unbalanced, to put it mildly:

> I do not wish to go on about all that has been done to my son since the start of the school year — you must already know. But you may be unaware of the insults and menaces which M. Simon subjected him to after class on Tuesday. Speaking of the position of fourth [out of eight] which he had given to René, Mr Simon

endeavored to show that he had made a great number of mistakes, 10 in fact [in his French composition] which is absurd and I can prove it and since he couldn't convince René he suggested that he choose one of the teachers, only from Nôtre Dame, as a judge, all this to the accompaniment of threats.... He added that M. Bossard had been perfectly right to stand up to him last year and he promised to do exactly the same this year. He said he also knew that although coming fourth made him ill, it would not give him typhoid fever, and finally, that he could go to the College or to Chailles or depart for distant shores and he would be glad to see the last of him....

It seems worth quoting these letters at some length as they indicate how highly strung the young Guénon and how tetchy his father were, how early in his life he found it very difficult to admit to having made mistakes, and how much he coveted coming first in everything he did. On October 23 the headmaster wrote in a conciliatory letter:

I am sad indeed, very sad, at the thought of seeing a child leave us, to whom as you know I have always shown, in every circumstance, the most fatherly affection and who for me is quite simply a victim of his own temperament — his excessive sensibility makes him see things quite differently to the way in which they really are.

This fact, the proof of which would far exceed the limits of an ordinary letter, does not in any way detract from René's good and fine qualities, which I and all the staff here recognize, but as I have already had occasion to point out to you, Sir, it is all up to him. And so he genuinely does believe that he is being persecuted, but this belief, based as it is on perpetual misunderstanding, is erroneous....

Obviously father and son shared a touchy and suspicious nature in addition to their very considerable intellectual abilities. A month later René's father wrote to the headmaster of Nôtre Dame announcing that he had put his son in the Collège Augustin-Thierry, whose staff and pupils, he believed, rejoiced in every kind of virtue.

The only member of the Nôtre Dame staff whom René admitted he was sorry to be parting from was his mathematics teacher, whom, he said, he would never forget. The letter concluded with the remark that his decision to remove René 'had nothing to do with René's impressionability.'

So in January 1902 René was enrolled as a student of rhetoric at a new school, the Collège Augustin-Thierry, a lay foundation with an excellent reputation in the town. The college was pleasantly situated facing the river in buildings that were formerly the Augustinian Abbey of Nôtre-Dame du Bourg-Moyer. During his first eight months at the new school, in spite of frequent bouts of ill-health which kept him at home, he did very well and by dint of hard work took part in the *Concours Générale* for Latin translation; in the following year he again took part in the philosophy and science examinations and was awarded a prize by the town for his work in physics. He passed the first part of his Baccalauréat with the citation 'satisfactory'. It was remarked that René had certain deficiencies in his work, once more in French composition and also in History and Geography.

But it was in philosophy that he shone and his teacher, Albert Leclère, described him as an excellent student. At the end of the year he won the college prize for excellence in Philosophy and a *Prix d'Honneur* for a French dissertation on a philosophical subject. He was also granted an *Accessit* in the Physics and Natural Sciences examinations and passed the second part of his Baccalauréat, again with the citation 'satisfactory'.

Continuing his studies, René showed himself particularly gifted in both mathematics and philosophy, which his tutor remarked he studied in an entirely disinterested way for its own sake. He was also picked out for his interest in religion and won a prize for religious instruction, as well as various other prizes and honorable mentions. During his three years at the college no signs of his hypersensitivity or feelings of persecution recurred, his health record improved, and—at least for his philosophy lectures under Albert Leclère—no record was made of his ever being absent.

There is no doubt that this distinguished teacher, who subsequently became a Professor of Philosophy in Switzerland and was himself deeply interested in the pre-Socratic philosophers, was a considerable influence in the formation of Guénon's thought. It is worth recalling that the first edition of Diehl's collection of the fragmentary remains of the pre-Socratic philosophers appeared in France in 1903. Leclère's first book, *Essai critique sur le droit d'affirmer,* has many passages suggestive of ideas Guénon was later to develop. J.P. Laurent instances his statement that 'all truth is first an opinion to which conviction becomes added as one fact to another.'[1] This emphasis on the reality of the metaphysical and the illusion of the phenomenal world was, from his earliest years, fundamental to Guénon's thought and he never abandoned it.

So this shy gangling young man, who had made few close friends but was intensely conscious of his own outstanding abilities, left school intending to obtain entry to one of the *Grande Écoles,* presumably hoping for an academic career and its attendant prestige, so much coveted in France. He enrolled as what is known in France as a mole (*taupe*) at the Collège Rollin; that is to say, as a student studying advanced mathematics to degree level. But something had changed; the model student of Blois became a far less satisfactory student in Paris, where he arrived in October 1904. Problems of ill-health and, one suspects, home-sickness beset him and he fell behind to such an extent that he had to have supplementary coaching. But in vain, for, as teachers said, he was 'still far from examination standard.' What was the reason for this failure? It was certainly not lack of ability. He had come with excellent recom-mendations from his school in Blois, but in the highly competitive atmosphere among selected students, and living in the hectic atmosphere of the Latin Quarter, all his old fears and delusions returned with renewed force as he realized he might fail in his endeavors. So in 1906, for reasons of health, Guénon left the hurly-burly of the Latin Quarter and installed himself in the little flat in the Île St Louis at 51 rue St Louis that was to be his home for the next 25 years.

Nothing could have been a greater change than this tranquil backwater that lies at the center of Paris, yet cut off from it on all sides by the river Seine. The rue St Louis en l'Île, to give it its full

---

1. *Le Sens caché dans l'oeuvre de René Guénon,* by J.P. Laurant (1975), p18.

name, is the main artery dividing the island in two, with numerous little lanes running off it on either side. Number 51 is still an impressive building dating from 1730 and formerly known as the Hôtel Cheniseau. The facade that fronts the street is typical of the period, with a large front door studded with metal bosses and an elaborate wrought-iron balcony above, supported by consoles in the shape of dragons and mascarons. There is a large interior courtyard at the bottom of which, on the right, a building of later date, several stories high, juts out. The various floors are served by a narrow and winding staircase. On the third floor at the end of a gloomy passage is the entrance to the little apartment that Guénon made his home until he left France for ever.

The spacious kitchen and dining room, which also served as a living room, were lit by gas, but the two bedrooms had to make do with lamps. The rooms were simply furnished and the salon had a piano, probably for the sake of his wife-to-be and the niece who came to live with them. Here Guénon was to lead a bachelor existence for some six years. He visited home frequently and stayed with his aunt, Madame Duru, who was teaching in a private school in a village called Montlivault. It was through her that he made his first contacts with the curé of the village, Abbé Ferdinand Gombault, and where he met his future wife, Berthe Loury, who taught in Madame Duru's school.

Guénon kept up his visits to Abbé Gombault right up to the time he left France for Egypt. Both of them were interested in the occult and in the findings of science relative to occult phenomena. But they approached such matters from very different points of view, the Abbé from that of rigid Catholic orthodoxy and the young Guénon from very receptive and open-minded interest. Gombault was concerned to reconcile the Bible with science. More congenial to Guénon's thought was the book he published in 1915 based on Genesis 11:1 ('Now the whole earth had one language and few words') called *Similitude des Écritures figuratives,* in which he endeavored to prove that Chinese, Egyptian, and Babylonian pictorial scripts had a common origin. He also agreed with Guénon in his mistrust of spiritualism.

Gombault's involvement with alleged apparitions at Tilly sur

Seilles and the undercurrents of satanic influences connected with them may have impressed the young Guénon with notions of satanic occult powers, which he retained throughout his life and which contributed to his notion of 'counter-initiation'.

Finally, Gombault's work *L'Imagination et les Phénomènes préternaturels* (1899), which Guénon certainly read with interest, was anti-Thomist in spirit and provided Guénon with refinements to the conventional body-mind-spirit triad. If we add to this the fact that Gombault was also interested in the borrowings made by Christianity and Judaism from Brahmanism, as he called the Vedanta philosophy, one can appreciate what a tremendous influence he had on Guénon. Many have commented on Guénon's remarkable memory, which, like Coleridge's, was 'tenacious and systematizing.' (J.P. Laurent has investigated the source of Guénon's ideas in considerable depth in his book *Le sens caché dans l'oeuvre de René Guénon.*)

The ground of all that was to follow had virtually been laid down by the time Guénon settled in his little flat. For the next six years he was to lead a busy bachelor life supported by visits from home and omelets cooked by his mother and sent up from Blois to ensure that he was getting enough to eat.

But those years were also to be ones of intense activity, intellectual exertion and research into the fascinating occult world which, since the days of Eliphas Lévi in the mid-nineteenth century, had formed a powerful element in the cultural life of Paris.

2

SEARCHING

Paul Chacornac in his *The Simple Life of René Guénon* calls the chapter on this period of Guénon's life 'In Search of the Lost Word'—in search of the 'lost word' of Freemasonry. Guénon's decision to retire from the highly competitive struggle for academic advancement was undoubtedly a crisis point in his life. It can be seen as a case of sour grapes ('If I can't be first I won't go on') or it can be seen, as I believe it should be, as the final rejection of the world and its values and the engagement on the lonely journey in search of an inner unchanging reality of which mathematics, and particularly geometry, were in some way the symbol. His interest in the pre-Socratic philosophers had been fired by his teacher at the Collège Augustin-Thierry, Albert Leclère. As we have seen, such pure and abstract thought had long been congenial to this shy young man. But first he had to explore the possibilities of there being available to him some attractive and more immediate means of access to this supreme knowledge, the password to which was the *parole perdue*. Such were the claims made by a host of fascinating and mysterious occult societies operating in Paris at that time. They offered ways forward that seemed much more attractive than the lectures of Bergson or the teachings of Auguste Comte that were much in vogue at that time.

One does not have to be much of a psychologist to see that this great interest in the occult was an expression of the romantic and emotional aspects of Guénon's personality which had otherwise been limited to devotion to his family and which needed further expression. Fragments of Guénon's earliest and unpublished writings of about this time include some romantic poetry and an unfinished novel on an occult theme.

In general it may be said that in the French, logical and rational tendencies are often balanced by a powerful emotional attachment to the ideals of a romantic nationalism in the form of a mystical belief in the supreme destiny of France; witness the cult of Joan of Arc and, more recently, of General de Gaulle. With this goes an avid interest in the mysterious, the mystical, the occult, the secret society, and a belief in the existence of a hidden network of influences, ever at work under the calm surface of everyday life; and quite often they seem to be proved right. Guénon himself was by no means altogether exempt from these tendencies.

Perhaps this attitude is fostered by the fact that France is a predominantly Catholic country and that the Church has always provoked resistance to its claims to infallibility and its sole possession of the means of salvation. Guénon himself shared a common ambivalent attitude towards the Church in that he admitted that, for the West, it was the means of preserving the Primordial Tradition, but for him personally it was easily abandoned in favor of Islam when circumstances made the change necessary.

The rejection of contemporary Christianity was one of the most powerful motives promoting interest in the occult, since most occult movements claimed to be in some sense Christian. They claimed to have the secrets of initiation, symbolism and ritual which Christianity had long neglected. Guénon frequently accused religion—and I think he had Christianity mainly in mind—of being sentimental and as appealing to emotions rather than to intellect. He would certainly have found much to support this view in the popular Catholicism of his day with its nauseating sentimentality over the Little Flower of Lisieux and popular devotion to the Sacred Heart of Jesus. Another attractive aspect of the occultism of the time was its claim to be in possession of the secrets of the mysterious East, notably from the Vedanta and from ancient Chinese sources.

There is a curious example of synchronicity which is worth noting. In October 1910 a serious young American also deeply interested in Vedanta philosophy came to Paris; he attended lectures by Bergson but there is no evidence that he contacted any occult groups, nor do we know if he had ever heard of René Guénon. His name was Tom Eliot, better known by his initials as T.S. Eliot.

Many were looking towards the East for enlightenment and in the evolution of this movement Guénon was to play an important part. But before he could do that he had to investigate the other and more immediately promising opportunities that were open to him. A friend introduced him to the leading figure in the occult world of that time. He was an energetic red-bearded doctor some 20 years older than Guénon called Gérard Encausse. He combined medical practice with vigorous proselytism for all aspects of the occult. He became a fluent and persuasive speaker and the list of his writings in his son's biography has more than a hundred and sixty entries of books, pamphlets and articles on every aspect of the occult: alchemy, Freemasonry, the kabbalah, astrology, divination, chiromancy, spiritualism, hypnotism, the elements of Sanskrit, Hebrew and Egyptian hieroglyphics, the Tarot, Rosicrucianism and so on. Like nearly all the occultists of the time he adopted an appropriate pseudonym and was widely known as Papus, a name taken from the *Nuctemeron* thought to be by Apollonius of Tyana. He was by far the most influential figure in the occult world of his day. He founded the review *L'Initiation*. He ran a school of occult studies called 'L'École supérieure libre des sciences hermétiques'. He revived earlier Martinist Orders based on the teachings of the eighteenth-century philosopher L.C. de Saint-Martin. He was co-founder of the Theosophical Society in France. He dabbled in fringe Masonry and pretty well every other branch of the hermetic sciences, extant or dormant, that he could find. He was decorated by the governments of Turkey and Portugal and in 1890 became an officer of the French Academy. He died in 1916, much respected and indeed revered by his contemporaries.

It was to Papus' School of Occult Studies that Guénon went on the recommendation of a college friend. Papus had himself been a student at the Collège Rollin in the 1880s and Victor-Emil Michelet tells us that he kept in touch with students long after he left.[1] His school arose out of an earlier group of friends and sympathizers called *Le Groupe indépendant d'études ésotériques*. The list of its members includes most of the noted occultists of the era, including

---

1. V.E. Michelet, *Les Compagnons de la Hiérophanie* (Paris, n.d.).

Péladan, Stanislas de Guaita, Barlet, Sédir, Marc Haven, and many others.

The two last-mentioned became instructors in the school and merit a word. Paul Sédir, whose real name was Yvon le Loup, was passionately interested in all occult studies. In his early years, having been given the freedom of Papus' extensive library, he wrote a number of important historical works of which the best was his *Histoire et Doctrines des Rose-Croix*, published in 1911. Later in life he was influenced by an extraordinary healer, Maître Philippe of Lyons, who combined great healing powers with extraordinary mystical-Christian insights. Sédir abandoned his occult studies and founded a non-denominational Christian society called *Les Amitiés Spirituelles,* which is still active today. The other teacher in Papus' school, Marc Haven, i.e., Dr Emmanuel Lalande, became the son-in-law of this same Maître Philippe, to whom he had been introduced by Papus. In later life he produced an edition of the *Tao Te Ching* and wrote on the Tarot and other occult subjects. The circle can be closed by recalling that in 1895 or thereabouts, when he was finishing his medical studies, Papus encouraged Maître Philippe to become the head of the *École pratique de Magnétisme* in Lyons, as a branch of the Parisian school founded by Hector Durville, a friend of Papus. Just before the Russian Revolution Papus and Maître Philippe were at the Court of the Tsar. Maître Philippe was eventually forced to leave due to the machinations of Rasputin. His powerful and mysterious spirit broods benevolently over the occult scene of the day and his views would certainly have been known to Guénon, though his fervent Christian mysticism would not have appealed to him.

There were two large, more or less public, organizations which appealed both to the general public and to occultists: the Spiritualist movement and the Theosophical Society. The Spiritualist movement originated in America with the phenomena produced by the Fox sisters in 1847–8. Spiritualism was a great success in the USA, the first general congress of spiritualists being held in Cleveland in 1852, and very shortly afterwards it arrived in France. The founder of French spiritualism was Hippolyte Rivail, a former pupil of Pestalozzi and a teacher in Lyons, that home of heterodox views. He took the name 'Allan Kardec', believing that he was the reincarnation of a Druid of that name. It is under this name that he is best known. He wrote a number of books, many of which are still in print and still studied in spite of their many failings. Spiritualism in France was in its early days much patronized by the Socialists of 1848, and the curious link between occult movements and a certain type of socialism was commented on by Guénon. It also attracted the strong body of *magnétiseurs* and hypnotists who had flourished in France since the days of Mesmer and le Marquis de Puységur at the end of the eighteenth century.

The Theosophical Society, founded by Madame H.P. Blavatsky and Colonel Olcott in New York in 1875, was spectacularly successful and soon reached France. Papus was an early admirer although later on he came to oppose it and exposed many of the shady goings-on in the Society. But it was, in spite of a strong element of charlatanry and constant internal dissension, the main vehicle for the dissemination of the idea that secret wisdom was available from the East, and its teachings were no doubt one element among those that led Guénon to study Eastern philosophy and religion.

In his first flush of enthusiasm, Guénon joined a number of occult organizations. In 1908 he took part in organizing a large Spiritualist-Masonic Congress but was known for his skepticism and left the platform at the very beginning of the meeting. In this year also he began to fall out with Papus, mainly because Guénon wished to revive the Order of the Temple, a fringe Masonic body that had never really got going. The following year he was introduced to Léonce Fabre des Essarts, an associate of Jules Doinel, creator in 1888 or 1889 of a revived Gnostic Church. This body came into existence as the result of a séance at Lady Caithness' house in which either the Albigensian Bishop Guillabert de Castres or the divine emanation of the Holy Aeons itself commanded Doinel to revive the ancient Gnostic Church. The first Synod of *L'Église Gnostique Universelle* was held in 1893 in 'La Librairie du Merveilleux', a popular rendezvous for occultists. Amongst those present were Lucien Chamuel, the owner of the bookshop, Albert de Pouvourville (Matgioi), Léon Champ-renaud, and Fabre des Essarts. On the retirement of Doinel, Fabre des Essarts took over the patriarchate. The Church was soon beset by internal feuds and a schism took place in 1899, with Jean Bricaud and a group in Lyons forming a rival Church.

These extraordinary bodies, in which everyone was a bishop or better, seem to us now extremely ludicrous, but they were taken seriously enough at the time. After the Bricaud schism, Albert de Pouvourville and Léon Champrenaud remained faithful to Fabre des Essarts. Albert de Pouvourville, better known by his pseudonym Matgioi, a name given to him when he was initiated into a Chinese Taoist secret society, had a powerful influence on Guénon. His initiation took place while he was a member of the French colonial service, stationed in Indo-China. He first met Guénon at the Spiritualist-Masonic Congress in 1908, in which year Guénon was consecrated Bishop in the neo-Gnostic Church with the name Palingenius, a play on his Christian name (René = reborn = Palingenius), no doubt on the suggestion of Matgioi. De Pouvourville had made translations of works by Lao Tzu and others and was a leading exponent of Taoist views at that time. His two major books *La Voie Métaphysique* (1905) and *La Voie Rationnelle* (1907) had a major influence on Guénon.

The third and most important element in the occult life of the time was Freemasonry, of which something must be said since it remained one of Guénon's great interests throughout his life.

Most people in Anglo-Saxon countries who are not Freemasons think of it as a queer secretive men's society with passwords and handclasps and a lot of strange rituals connected with the square and the compass, the plumb-line and Solomon's Temple. It is seen to be pretty harmless, a good thing to be in from the point of view of business and social contacts and a source of help if you get into difficulties. Masons are said to look after one another, and stories are told like that of the judge who received a Masonic sign from the prisoner in the dock before him and promptly let him off. In any event they do a lot a charitable work and members include royalty and presidents, as well as Anglican clergymen—even bishops and archbishops.

Every now and then a scare is raised, a sensational book is published, the police are told not to join, and a few clergymen leave the Church of England for Rome under the impression that the

Catholic Church is passionately opposed to Masonry. Such is the public perception of Masonry in England and America.

In France the perception is very different. For one thing it is taken much more seriously. Many Catholics believe it to be entirely evil. Funerals of Masons are forbidden in Catholic churches and in obituary notices clear distinctions are made between Church members and Masons. Its tenets are debated on radio and television, anti-Masonic societies and periodicals abound. Masonry has often been the cover under which political opposition sheltered. It has often been violently anti-clerical and has often clashed with the Jesuits who, when public opinion was raised against *them*, were accused of being secretly in league with Masonry. Within Masonry itself there have been numerous splits, schisms, divisions, reunions, and reformations, which seem in some ways to be the mirror image of the Christian Church in the West.

Guénon was naturally enough attracted to certain fringe Masonic groups since many Masons were also members of other esoteric groups. Guénon contacted *La Loge symbolique Humanidad* (*du Rite national espagnol*) whose venerable head was Charles Detré, known as Teder, an associate of Papus. Teder had been exiled from France in 1884 for his liberal opinions, landing up in England, where he edited an emigré paper *Le Moniteur des Consulats*. He later settled in Nottingham, where he lived for twenty-five years. He became friendly with John Yarker, whom Ellic Howe describes as a 'notorious promoter of bogus Masonic rites.' In 1906 he returned to Paris and became a member of the staff of Papus' school, where he seems to have done much as his friend Yarker did in the promotion of dubious rites, such as *La Grande Loge Swedenborgienne de France* and the re-established *Rite de Memphis-Misraïm*, as well as *La Loge symbolique Humanidad*, into which he received the young Guénon.

Guénon's other contact with Masonry at this time was with another colorful and equally dubious character, Theodore Reuss (1855–1923). Reuss really merits a full biography. Son of an innkeeper in Augsburg, he began his extraordinary career as a commercial traveler. In 1876 he was in England where he joined a Masonic lodge, the Pilgerloge, most of whose members were Germans. After a visit to Germany, where he discovered Wagner's music, he returned to England and endeavored to popularize Wagner by organizing not very successful concerts. Being hard up for cash, he turned to journalism, taking a great interest in English politics and joining William Morris's Socialist League. He also became deeply involved in Anarchist and Communist circles and did not stay long with Morris. At the same time he joined a number of occult societies, including the Theosophical Society, and some of the Masonic rites of John Yarker, whom he knew. Like all such people, he wanted to have his own order, so he founded the OTO (Ordo Templum Orientis) and became a member of the Hermetic Order of the Golden Dawn. His later history, though fascinating, does not concern us here. Reuss received Guénon into something called 'The Chapter and Temple INRI of the Primitive and Original Swedenborgian Rite' and immediately invested him with the 30th grade: Chevalier Kadosch.

By 1909 Guénon had had enough of this tomfoolery and turned his back on it. Spiritualism and Theosophy he saw through very quickly and ably demolished their pretensions to be taken seriously in two large books. Summing up his thoughts on the whole neo-spiritualist movement, he wrote in *La Gnose* for December 1909 as follows:

> It is impossible to make a coherent whole of such widely differing doctrines as those which may be included under the name of Spiritualism. Such materials can never be used to construct a stable building. Where most of the so-called Spiritualist doctrines are at fault is that they are really materialism trans-posed to a different plane, and wish to apply the methods used by science in studying the material world, to the spiritual realm. These experimental methods will never enable us to understand anything but simple phenomena on the basis of which it is impossible to construct any metaphysical theory. Besides, the pretension that we can acquire knowledge of the spiritual world by material means is obviously absurd. It is within ourselves alone that we can discover the principles of this knowledge and not in external objects.

We know clearly, then, what Guénon thought of the claims of Theosophy and Spiritualism and how little of authentic truth he found in them. But what did he think about all the other bodies and groups that he participated in with such apparent lack of discrimination?

We know that he thought of writing a third volume exposing the flaws of those aspects of the occult establishment not covered in the first two, and we may well feel sorry that he did not do so. All these groups were in some way or another connected with the parent stem of orthodox Masonry. But however far removed from that stem they may have been, and however much they owed their origin, not to any legitimate affiliation with genuinely initiatic bodies, but to the egotism of their inventors, he nevertheless felt that what they were attempting was valuable. I suspect that he would for the most part have considered them as inept follies rather than as dangerous errors. Be that as it may, from now on he concentrated on what he increasingly saw as his life work. This could perhaps be summed up as one of warning and enlightening. First of all, the West had to be warned that it was heading for destruction, and secondly, it must be made clear that it was only by the rediscovery of, and adherence to, the one universal, immutable, primordial tradition that new life could emerge out of the ruins of the old.

3

FINDING

About this time others beside Guénon were finding the ebullient superficiality and the all-embracing welcome given by Papus to every manifestation new and old of the occult increasingly uncongenial. Chief among them were two of his most prominent associates whom we have already mentioned, Léon Champrenaud (1870–1925) and, to give him his full title, Albert Puyou, Comte de Pouvourville (1862–1939).

Champrenaud had from his youth been active in the occult movement, but became increasingly dissatisfied with it. From exactly which of his many contacts he derived his interest in Sufi mysticism is not clear, but it seems likely that it was stimulated by another of those strange figures who so often crop up on the occult scene. In 1890 a young Swedish painter, Ivan Gustaf Aguéli, to give him the version of his name he adopted in France, arrived in Paris and joined the studio of Emile Bernard, a well-known artist of the time. Aguéli was another who showed interest in both the occult and extreme left-wing politics since he joined the Theosophical Society and became intimate with anarchist circles in Paris.

On his second visit in 1892 he formed a liaison with a like-minded girl, by name Marie Huot, who was also a Theosophist and a Socialist. Aguéli was held in jail for several months for harboring an anarchist wanted by the police. During his time in prison he studied Hebrew and Arabic besides reading such writers as Fabre d'Olivet, Dionysius the Areopagite, Villiers, l'Îsle Adam, and, not surprisingly, his compatriot Swedenborg.

On his release he spent two years in Egypt and then returned to study oriental languages at the *École des Langues Orientales*. In 1897 he appears to have become a practising Muslim, while still being deeply interested in Buddhism, an interest which led him to make an abortive attempt to reach the then forbidden city of Lhasa. In 1902 we find him once more in Paris contributing to *La Revue Blanche* and *L'Initiation*. But he was ever on the move and with a young Italian doctor he went to Egypt hoping to bring about mutual understanding between East and West. While he was in Egypt he was initiated into a Sufi *ṭarīqah* under the name of Abdul-Hādi by the Shaykh 'Abd al-Raḥmān 'Ilaysh al-Kabir. In 1909 he returned to Paris, authorized by the Shaykh to initiate people into the Sufi movement.

'Abd al-Raḥmān 'Ilaysh al-Kabir, who was Aguéli's *pir*, or spiritual father, was the restorer of the Maliki rite, dominant in West Africa and the Sudan. He was the son of an even more famous spiritual leader of the same name who had been imprisoned by the British in Egypt at the time of the revolt of Arabi Pasha. The particular brand of Sufism that they taught was based on the teachings of one of the greatest of all Muslim Sufis, Ibn Arabi, who was born in Spain in 1165 and studied in Seville. His doctrine is founded on the *Kalām* or *Logos*, which, as G.C. Anawati writes, 'can be envisaged in three ways: ontologically, mystically, and mythically.'[1] The myth was that of the Perfect Man. It is easy to see how much of this teaching remained with Guénon throughout his life and how congenial it is to his way of thought. The following year Aguéli met Guénon, who had just founded a little periodical called *La Gnose* in which he shared the burden of writing with Champrenaud and Pouvourville. *La Gnose* included a considerable part of Guénon's *Symbolism of the Cross*, which, when it appeared in book form, was dedicated to ''Abd al-Raḥmān 'Ilaysh al-Kabir to whom I owe the first idea of this book' and is obviously deeply influenced by Guénon's study of the teachings of Ibn Arabi. The following year Guénon was initiated by Aguéli into the Sufi *ṭarīqah*, by receiving the *barakah* or blessing at his hands. He adopted the name of Shaykh 'Abd al-Wahed Yahia. This event, which he did not publicize at the time and which did not seem to disturb his external adherence to Christianity, was eventually to lead him to open confession of Islam.

---

1. George C. Anawati, *The Legacy of Islam* (1974), chap. 8, 'Philosophy, Theology, and Mysticism'.

Guénon and Aguéli continued to collaborate and made ambitious schemes for the translation of all the important Sufi mystical texts. This was a project long cherished by Guénon who only abandoned it after the débacle of his visit to Cairo twenty years later with Madame Dina. But for the moment the four friends were collaborating closely on *La Gnose,* to which all of them contributed. Aguéli, in the issue for January 1911, wrote an important article on the doctrinal identity of Taoism and Islam in which he used Matgioi's expositions of Taoism as the basis for Taoism alongside his own understanding of Islam.

Guénon's interest in Hindu doctrines had no doubt been aroused by his contacts with the Theosophical Society, which was ostensibly linked to Indian philosophical teachings, though much adulterated by Madame Blavatsky's eclectic additions from a host of other sources, and as such soon rejected by Guénon.

But Vedanta was very much in the air at that time, mainly due to the activities of Swami Vivekananda, who had attended the Parliament of Religions in Chicago in 1893 as a representative of Hinduism and whose writings had been widely read in America and Europe.

Guénon always claimed that he received his teachings orally from Hindu and other masters and there certainly were Hindu teachers in Paris about this time; but it has not been possible to establish from which, if any of them, Guénon actually received his teaching, although there is no reason to doubt the truth of his statement.

In general he was noticeably reticent about his sources, but we learn of discussions held in his little flat late into the night in which his closest friends regularly took part, along with a stream of passing visitors of all kinds, Muslims, Hindus, and others. But there were two French contemporaries, and friends, who also no doubt influenced him. One was Sédir (Yvon Le Loup), of whom we have already spoken, who had made a deep study of Vedanta philosophy and had eventually rejected it in favor of a Christian mysticism. In his work on the Rosicrucian Movement, *Les Rose-Croix,* Sédir speaks very highly of Guénon but takes issue with him over his extreme abstract and impersonal point of view which, in Sédir's view, ignores the world, mankind, and love and suffering in favor of a metaphysical endeavor to transcend them.[2] Sédir himself had studied Vedanta and no doubt encouraged his students in Papus' *École Hermétique* to do so also. The other influence was a somewhat mysterious character, Alexandre St Yves d'Alveydre (1842–1909), who in the 1870s and 1880s had written a number of philosophical and kabbalistic works culminating in a vast work, *L'Archéométrie*, which described a new social system which he called *Synarchie*—a highly idiosyncratic amalgam of current esoteric ideas with notions derived from Fourier and Le Play. It is indicative of the persistence of these ideas that most of d'Alveydre's works are still in print and that *Synarchie* still has its adherents; during the Second World War it was even used as a cover for a curious and elusive international conspiracy that received attention from the British Secret Service.[3]

But the main works by d'Alveydre which influenced Guénon were *Clefs de l'Orient* (1877), reprinted several times, in which Guénon's ideas concerning the élite may be found as well as ideas of a Primordial Tradition, and *La Mission de l'Inde*, in which, as Jean Saunier points out, there are suggestions developed by Guénon in *The King of the World* concerning a mysterious Center known as Agarttha, where the King of the World resides.

The basic concepts acquired by Guénon during this period were in fact the basis on which he built all his work, and he did not really develop any significantly new ideas after that date. In 1912, the year he was secretly initiated into the Muslim *ṭarīqah* by Aguéli, he also got married to a young schoolmistress, an assistant to his aunt Madame Duru. The marriage was conducted in the normal Catholic way and to all outward appearances Guénon was still a Catholic. Madame Duru, and later a young niece, came to share the little flat with the young couple. They were very hard up and Guénon had to count the *sous* very carefully. The bachelor years were over and with them, I think, any further fundamental changes in Guénon's basic assumptions. From now on he was to expound them and to defend them, but not substantially to change them.

2. Paul Sédir, *Les Rose-Croix* (Paris, 1972).
3. G. de Charnay, *Synarchie Panorama de 25 années d'activité occulte* (Paris, 1946).

4

CUTTING THE TIES

From now on Guénon's life was to change both out-wardly and inwardly. Outwardly because he now had family respon-sibilities and had to earn a living, and inwardly because he had become increasingly disillusioned with the occult establishment of his time.

He retained his interest in Masonry and in the same year as his marriage he confirmed his affiliation to the Thebah Lodge associated with *La Grande Loge de France* of the ancient and accepted Scottish Rite. Yet in the following year we find him associating with one of the leading anti-Masonic writers of the time, Abel Clarin de la Rive (1855–1914). In order to understand what lies behind this, it is necessary to know a little about the violent war that had been waged throughout the nineteenth century between the Church and Freemasonry.

Continental Masonry, as we have seen, was very different from its English parent. In England the Church and the Masons soon settled down to an amiable co-existence. Not so in France, where after the first half-century of friendly cooperation, when laity and clergy felt no difficulty in being Masons, post-revolutionary France became polarized and a strong anti-clerical rationalist opposition faced a beleaguered and increasingly hard-line Church.

French Masonic Lodges became the refuge of anti-clerical and radical reformers of all sorts and were also infiltrated by occultists of various persuasions, from outside as well as inside France; all of which was known or suspected by many. Rumors and hints were rife and many young people were attracted to the combination of mystery and radical political views that seemed to be found in Masonry. Amongst those so drawn was a young man named Gabriel Jogand, the son of a very clerically connected family of Marseille. He was still a student at a Jesuit college when he first became interested in Masonry. At the age of fourteen he ran away to join an exiled radical, Henri Rochefort, in Belgium. He was arrested at the frontier and on the request of his father, sent to a reformatory. The young boy never forgot or forgave his family, or the Church, whom he blamed equally for the severe punishment he received. Again he ran away from home and went with a regiment of Zouaves to Algiers. Brought back, more rebellious than ever, he took part in the Commune of 1870 and began writing for various radical papers, adopting the pseudonym by which he is generally known, Léo Taxil.

In 1878 he moved to Paris to start an anti-clerical paper and to arouse enough interest to enable him to found an anti-clerical political party. This same year he was invited to a Masonic festival in Béziers and subsequently joined a Lodge in Paris. But the Masons of the Grand Orient soon became alarmed at his reckless anti-clericalism and mocking attitude even to Masonic rituals.

In 1884 Leo XIII issued his famous Bull *Humani Generis* condemning Masonry. This same year the volatile and unstable revolutionary Taxil repented and changed his tune completely and used his fertile pen to produce a stream of anti-Masonic pamphlets, including one suggesting that Pope Pius IX was a Freemason. The most famous of these works was an extensive exposé, *Le Diable au XIXème siècle* (1892–5), in which he made references to diabolical and satanist rites practiced by Masons and which he called Palladism. His final fling was to produce a work alleged to be written by a certain repentant participant in Satanic Masonic rites, Diana Vaughan, who never existed outside Taxil's imagination. Many were deceived; but eventually, suspected and shunned by all at an anti-Masonic Congress in Trent in 1896, he confessed that Diana Vaughan had never existed and the whole anti-Masonic scare collapsed. Taxil lived on until 1907, supporting himself by various degrading forms of hack journalism.

One of those who at first believed him was Abel Clarin de la Rive, a convinced but reasonable anti-Masonic propagandist. On the final exposure of Taxil and Diana Vaughan, Clarin de la Rive took over from him the editorship of the leading anti-Masonic paper, *La*

France chrétienne antimaçonnique. Clarin de la Rive was extremely interested in Islam and had become something of an expert on the subject, even to the extent of being thought by some to *be* a Muslim. He used the pages of his paper to publish a series of articles on North African Muslim secret societies.

Ten years after this Guénon caught the attention of the older man through his contributions to *La Gnose,* one of which de la Rive reprinted in its entirety in his journal. Guénon soon began writing regularly for it. Marie-France James states that on Clarin de la Rive's death Guénon would have certainly been offered the editorship if the 1914–18 war had not intervened.[1] Many have commented adversely on Guénon's apparent duplicity in writing for an anti-Masonic paper while at the same time being a member of a Masonic Lodge. Two things need to be remembered. One was that Guénon was always his own man and his approach to Masonry was always idealistic. This being so, he saw clearly that Masonry suffered the same falling away from its original initiatory and symbolic heritage and had degenerated in much the same way as the Catholic Church. So Guénon felt free to attack the rationalistic anti-spiritual Masonry of his time which had abolished all references to the 'Great Architect of the Universe' and was highly politicized and anti-clerical in tone. His position was much the same as that of a sincere Catholic who writes in a Protestant paper attacking the errors and abuses of the Church he loves. There seems to me no doubt that in spite of all his disillusionments and disappointments Guénon remained convinced of the importance of Masonry as a transmitter of the Primordial Tradition. As Paul Chacornac points out, Guénon never stopped attacking the malicious distortions and misrepresentations of certain anti-Masonic writers following in Taxil's footsteps. For example, in 1929, in a review of an anti-Masonic novel *L'Élue du Dragon* which purported to be the memoirs of a certain Clothilde Bersone, a highly-placed member of a *Grande Loge des Illuminés,* Guénon points out how this is a rehash of the old Diana Vaughan fictions and so should be totally disregarded. A little

---

1. Marie-France James, *Ésotérisme et Christianisme autour de René Guénon* (Paris, 1981), pp 105 ff.

later on he speaks of a sympathetic writer, Léon de Poncin, who quoted him extensively and whose sympathetic treatment 'is an agreeable change for us from the insults and the hate-filled displays of certain other anti-Masons.'

In a long review of L. Fry's *Léo Taxil et la Franc-maçonnerie*, he once again attacks the neo-Taxilians and their misrepresentation either through malice or ignorance of perfectly well-known Masonic facts in order to make out a case for the existence of satanism and luciferian practices which, as Guénon says, no doubt exist but have nothing to do with Masonry. Many more examples could be quoted. For those who want more proof, they will find it in the two volumes of Guénon's writings on Masonry.

But now, in following his life, we must turn from his collaboration with *La France Anti-maçonnique* to his other contacts and experiences. During the First World War he was exempted from military service on account of his poor health. Since his father's death in 1913 he had a small personal income that was perforce reduced during the war. As a result he had to take up teaching in order to make ends meet. He taught in St Germain-en-Laye for the school year 1915–16 and the following year in Blois, where he was glad to be near his mother, who died in March 1917 after a long and painful illness. In September 1917 Guénon was appointed lecturer in philosophy at Setif in Algeria. When he started work there in October he found to his chagrin that he was also expected to teach elementary French and Latin. But at least he had time to improve his knowledge of Arabic, and life was made easier for him by the presence of Dr Lesueur, an old friend from Blois who had married a pupil of Madame Duru and thus also knew Berthe Guénon.

In October 1918 he returned to France and settled with his wife and his aunt in the old family home in Blois. Soon afterwards he was appointed lecturer in philosophy at his old school, the Collège Augustin-Thierry. The school buildings at that time were being used as an American ambulance station, so teaching was beset with difficulties. His wife shared in all his work. Not having any children they adopted a niece, Françoise Belile, whom Guénon taught and also greatly spoilt. They returned to their apartment in Paris in 1919. During the early years of the war Guénon, with his friend Pierre

Germain, had attended classes in philosophy, and in 1916 Germain introduced him to a young girl student, Noële Maurice-Denis, who in turn introduced Guénon to the circle of brilliant young philosophy students who had gathered round Fr Emile Peilleaube, doyen of the Faculty of Philosophy of the *Institut catholique de Paris*. The brightest of all these students was undoubtedly Jacques Maritain. According to Noële Maurice-Denis, by this time Guénon had ceased to be the wild occult experimenter of former years and was now 'a young bourgeois uniquely passionate in the cause of truth and intellectualism.'[2] During 1916 Guénon and Maritain corresponded frequently on philosophy and metaphysics, but they never succeeded in reconciling their differences. In 1917 he started a similar correspondence with Noële Maurice-Denis, and while she was more sympathetic than Maritain neither of them could persuade Guénon to adopt their brand of neo-Thomism. Once more Guénon was to prove obdurately that he was his own man, though at the end of her life Maurice-Denis wrote that

> apart from the questions of terminology which were impossible to reconcile, Guénon's position in pure metaphysics was nearer to the Thomist position than that professed by any modern thinkers, Christian or not.

During this time Guénon was also working on his first published book, *Introduction to the Study of the Hindu Doctrines*. He had submitted the text to Silvain Lévi as a thesis for a doctorate, but it was refused. Reading it now one can easily understand why, since it fails to display the sort of academic documentation and 'even-handedness' required in such theses. Nevertheless, with the help of Fr Peilleaube, the work *was* accepted by the publisher Rivière and duly appeared.

Noële Maurice-Denis, writing long afterwards in an article on Guénon in *La Pensée Catholique* (1962), looked back on her friend of nearly forty years and gave the impression that, though Guénon had abandoned the search for truth among the occultists, he was not drawn towards the Christianity of the neo-Thomists. The stumbling

2. M.-F. James, loc. cit., p165.

block was not only 'vocabulary' but also a tempera-mental and deep-seated rejection of all affective thinking, which in Christianity, even in its most intellectual presentation, is always prominent. Guénon could not bring himself to accept that the high-est form of knowledge was to be obtained by the union of the mind and the feelings, the union of intellect with love. This being so, he rejected mysticism as a valid way and insisted on following his lonely path of pure intellectual intuition as being the only way to transcend human limitations and to be reunited with the Principial Unity. This was to be his *qismat,* his destiny, and eventually to lead him to his resting place in the house of Islam.

5

BREAKING LOOSE

GUÉNON'S LIFE FROM NOW on became increasingly lived in his head and in his writings, and in discussions with friends in the evenings in his flat on the Île St Louis. The year 1921 saw the publication of his large book on Theosophy, *Theosophy: History of a Pseudo-Religion,* much of which had appeared in the *Revue de Philosophie.* The work is exceedingly well documented and although much more is now known about the ludicrous and fantastic side of the movement, Guénon's book is still worth reading. It reveals clearly how little he was deceived but always remained skeptical about the claims of the Society—an attitude which we may infer was adopted towards the other occult societies and organizations with which he came into contact.

Paul Chacornac, who ran a bookshop specializing in occult literature, has a clear recollection of a January morning in 1922 when he saw a man come into the shop,

> very tall and thin with brown hair, round about thirty years old, dressed in black, in appearance a classic example of a French intellectual university type. His elongated face with a thin moustache was lightened by clear, strangely piercing eyes which gave the impression that they saw behind the surface of things.[1]

He had come to sell books, accumulated while writing on Theosophy, which he no longer required. It was the beginning of a friendship which lasted for the rest of his life. When Chacornac went round to the little apartment, he was struck by the life-size portrait

---

1. Paul Chacornac, *La Vie Simple de René Guénon* (Paris, 1982); English translation, *The Simple Life of René Guénon* (Ghent, NY: Sophia Perennis, in press).

hanging on the wall of a Hindu woman dressed in red velvet, and on the mantelpiece an eighteenth-century Masonic clock. A piano and bookshelves overflowing with books completed the décor. From Chacornac we get a glimpse of Guénon's home life. His wife Berthe was an excellent musician and used to play the piano quietly while Guénon read, which he much enjoyed. Some-times they would go to concerts together, though more often Guénon would be at his desk working. He was far from being a solitary (he also gave private lessons), but his main occupation was writing; his wife was his sub-editor and secretary, helping in the preparation of his books. Her brother told Marie-France James that without her help Guénon's works might never have been published.

Two of his most intimate friends at this time were Dr Tony Grangier, who was his own doctor, and Frans Vreede, who got him a part-time job in the library of the *Center d'Études néerlandaises* in the University of Paris. Vreede was a Dutchman who came from the University of Leiden to Paris for postgraduate work studying Romance languages. He soon became close to Guénon, whose interests he shared, particularly his interest in Eastern philosophy.

In 1926 he was, with Guénon, instrumental in founding a small society, *L'Union intellectuelle pour l'entente des Peuples,* which continued to exist until Guénon left France in 1931. Vreede's future career took him to India and then to Java, where he became a member of the Dutch Grand Orient Lodge of Java. When the Japanese invaded the island, he was made a prisoner of war and on his release became the first Professor of French in the University of Indonesia. In 1953 he published his major work, *Essentials of Living Hindu Philosophy,* in the revision of which he had been helped by Guénon. Another personal friend whose recollections of Guénon are both sympathetic and perceptive was Gonzague Truc. For instance, he noted that Gué-non in conversation never used the word 'I', a fact which those who read his books carefully will also note. Truc rightly points to Guénon's single-mindedness as purity of intention. He allowed, says Truc, no considerations of academic advancement or personal benefit to interfere with his work. He disdained academic neglect and personal attacks, which simply reinforced his determination to back his views with the greatest possible intellectual and scholarly support. But such was his modesty and unwillingness to parade his knowledge that he rarely quotes any secondary sources and repeatedly points to the pure message that he transmits as being all-important. His own personal endorsement or the supporting evidence of others he deemed irrelevant.

Truc was for some time editorial adviser to the publishers Bossard, and by his intervention they published two of Guénon's major works, *Man and His Becoming according to the Vedānta* in 1925 and *The Crisis of the Modern World* in 1927. Previous to these Guénon had published *The Spiritist Fallacy* in 1923 and *East and West* in 1924. He was of necessity gaining some readers, but was very largely ignored both by the general public and academic and intellectual circles.

In 1924 Frederic Lefèvre, editor-in-chief of the prestigious journal *Les Nouvelles Littéraires*, decided to hold a press conference centered on a recently published and rather sensational travel book by the Polish writer, Ferdinand Ossendowski, called *Beasts, Men and* Gods. René Grousset, an acknowledged expert on China, Jacques Maritain, a leading Christian neo-Thomist, and René Guénon, as an expert on Hinduism, were invited to take part. Ossendowski claimed to have visited a mysterious wise man in Mongolia who corresponded in many respects to the legendary King of the World, residing in his capital Agarttha at the center of the world. In the discussion, the existence of such a person and place were really secondary to the inescapable difference of opinion between the participants as to how East and West should relate to one another. Guénon saw the way forward as a harmonious dissemination of Eastern ideas in the West which would enable it to recover the Primordial Tradition, once enshrined in the Catholic Church but now almost entirely lost and visible only in a very degenerate form. Maritain saw any such movement as leading to the inevitable subordination and eventual destruction of the Christian faith as enshrined in the Catholic Church. This revealed faith could not give first place to what for Guénon went far beyond it, namely 'true and authentic metaphysical wisdom.' Once more the sticking point was the concept of love as the highest wisdom as opposed to the impersonal 'pure intellectual intuition' of Guénon and Eastern philosophies.

One more major event in Guénon's life in France must be recorded, and that is his relationship with the journal *Regnabit,* edited by Fr Felix Anizan (1878–1944) and founded in 1920 in conjunction with the center at Paray-le-Monial dedicated to the promotion of devotion to the Sacred Heart of Jesus. The link between Fr Anizan and Guénon was their mutual friend Louis Charbonneau-Lassay (1881–1946), an archaeologist of note who through his religious upbringing was also interested in Christian symbolism. Charbonneau-Lassay was a member of a society devoted to the Sacred Heart and took part in the Eucharistic Congress at Paray-le-Monial in 1921. He contributed many articles on symbolism in *Regnabit* and in 1934 he completed his *magnum opus, Le Bestiaire du Christ.*[2] He was for Guénon the final authority on all matters relating to symbolism.

Regnabit and the cult of devotion to the Sacred Heart were always controversial. Both Fr Anizan and his wealthy backer Baron Alexis de Sarachaga were on the margin of orthodoxy and sometimes overstepped it. The cult of devotion to the Sacred Heart acquired political and nationalist overtones. Sarachaga has been described as a Naundorffist, by which is implied that he was a Royalist and longed for the restoration of the monarchy. Alongside this nostalgia for the historical past of France went a similar nostalgia for 'a renewal of the primitive revelation under the sovereign rule of Christ,' to quote the words of Baron de Rosnay in his book *Le Hiéron du Val d'Or élevé en hommage à Jésus Hostie-Roi.* The Hiéron, a Greek word meaning a sacred enclosure, was the name given to the elaborate complex of buildings at Paray-le-Monial which includes a library and museum devoted to the cult of the Sacred Heart.

Guénon's participation in *Regnabit* was terminated by the hostility, he believed, of certain neo-scholastic circles. This was the last of his attempts to find a circle or group who would accept him and allow him the complete independence and freedom without which he could not function. In 1925 he gave his only public lecture, on *Eastern Metaphysics,* or rather, he explained, 'the metaphysics without a name, since it is neither Eastern nor Western but universal.'

---

2. Partially translated as *The Bestiary of Christ* (NY: Parabola Books, 1991).

From 1924 onwards Guénon had supplemented his income by giving special lessons and courses of philosophy in a private girls' school near his flat. One cannot help admiring the patient and uncomplaining way in which he undertook the teaching necessary to make ends meet. The fact that the girls, whose parents were comfortably off, were none of them highly motivated to study must have made the work very irksome.

Nevertheless, he continued writing books and articles, including a number of book reviews. In 1927 he published two important books, *The King of the World*, an outcome of a conference on Ossendowski, and *The Crisis of the Modern World*, and in 1929 the outstanding *Spiritual Authority and Temporal Power*, and also his small pamphlet on *St Bernard*, author of the Statutes of the Order of Templars.

He did not publish anything in 1928 and the reason is not hard to find. In January of that year his beloved wife Berthe died of spinocerebral meningitis and nine months later Madame Duru, his support and companion from childhood, also died. One further blow was that his niece Françoise, whom he loved dearly, also had to leave him. He took this triple blow with characteristic fortitude. For a short time he was devastated and showed it. For a while he did exhibit some signs of a return to the old persecution mania, but then he covered it up and spoke no more about it. But as his old friend Gonzague Truc noticed and recorded in the memorial issue of *Études Traditionnelles* published in 1951 after Guénon's death:

> The seriousness of the blow can be judged by its result. The wound compelled him towards some distant sanctuary and in these events we can discern the determining factors behind his departure.

The separation between Françoise Belile and her uncle was painful for both of them and, in her case, may have been one factor in her eventual entry into the religious life under the name of Sister Marie-Chantal. His friends rallied round him, hoping to keep him within the Catholic fold, but seemingly the die was cast and events were leading him implacably away from Paris and towards the East.

6

TURNING TO MECCA

Like many men of letters and intellectuals, Guénon was not cut out to be a bachelor; he needed the support of a wife and a secure home background. Soon after Berthe's death he made a tentative attempt at a second marriage with a partner chosen from among his circle of friends, but his offer was refused. But early in 1930 his three friends, Dr Grangier, Mario Meunier, and François Pierrepeu, were together when Guénon burst in on them late at night obviously very excited. He announced that he was soon going to Egypt in company with a certain Madame Dina, the widow of an Egyptian engineer. Madame Dina was a Canadian by birth and wealthy, having inherited a considerable fortune from her father, a railway tycoon. Her husband, also wealthy, had died the previous year on his way back from India.

Madame Dina and Guénon had met some time previously in Chacornac's bookshop. They had become friends, had traveled to Alsace together, and then spent some time on a property she owned at Cruzeilles in Haute-Savoie. It is not difficult to understand how the two bereaved people were attracted to one another. They planned to found a publishing house, *Editions Véga*, and to publish a collection of translations of original texts illustrating the Primordial Tradition as exemplified by the various religions.

This was the motive for their trip to Egypt, where they hoped to collect a large number of Sufi texts for translation and publication by the new company. They left on March 5. By the end of only three months Madame Dina had returned, and soon after married Ernest Britt, a member of an occult circle hostile to Guénon. The plans for the publishing house and the issue of the series of texts soon folded; the publishing house later passed out of Madame Dina's control and the series of translations was eventually abandoned by the new management.

Guénon did not immediately decide never to return to France. At first he spoke of return as a possibility 'when the time was ripe.' He lived a modest life with minimum contacts with Western expatriates. He perfected his Arabic and in 1931 published a series of articles in an Arab periodical, *Al-Marifah*.

He renewed his contacts with the Shadhili Sect and attended meetings held by Shaykh Salama Radi, whom he had met at the Seyidna al-Hussein mosque. He moved from his original lodging to a modest apartment over a confectioner's shop opposite the al-Azhar university. From the beginning he abandoned Western clothes and adopted the current Egyptian style of dress, and of course now openly used his initiatic name of 'Abd al-Wahed Yahia.

At first he was very hard up and may even at times have gone short of food; but gradually his situation improved and he became more organized and began writing for his friend Chacornac's periodical *Études Traditionnelles*, for which he regularly provided reviews of books and articles, as well as contributing a number of articles on symbolism and other subjects.

In 1934 he married the eldest daughter of Shaykh Mohammed Ibrahim, the lawyer who had handled his affairs, and the newlywed couple went to live with the bride's parents. In June 1935 he finally decided to sell his apartment in the Île St Louis. This decision must, in some sense, have marked his final break with his homeland and his determination to spend the rest of his life in Egypt. When the sale of the apartment in Paris was complete he moved house yet again to slightly more spacious quarters in al-Azhar street. In July of this year he took a short holiday in Alexandria with his wife, probably to collect the books, papers and other belongings he had had sent out from Paris on giving up his flat there.

After his father-in-law's death in 1937 the couple moved again to a comfortable bourgeois house in a quiet suburb with a distant view of the pyramids. In 1939 one of his admirers, John Levy, a wealthy English Jew who had become a Muslim, bought Guénon's house and gave it to him as a token of his appreciation. For reasons not now clear, the family moved back into the center of Cairo in 1946, occupying a house in Gam'a Abedine street near the Royal Palace. His first child, named Khadija, was born in 1944, and the second, another daughter, Leila, in 1946, his first son, Ahmed, in 1949, and another son, 'Abd al-Wahed, in 1951, after his father's death.

Guénon's life in Cairo and his contact with Paris and *Études Traditionnelles* in particular were greatly eased by his young friend Maurice Clavelle, known as Jean Reyor, who acted as an intermediary between Guénon and the many people who wanted to contact him. His life in Cairo was mainly occupied in study and writing; over the years he carried on an increasingly extensive correspondence with people from all over the world who wrote to him for advice on philosophical and religious matters; he often wrote over fifty letters a week. It is greatly to be hoped that some of these letters may be collected and published. He was noticeably kinder and more friendly in his correspondence than he was in his published reviews.

His friends in France were at first anxious to know how and why he was living in Cairo, being unaware of his open profession of Islam. Hearing of his straitened circumstances, some of them sent money to him through the diplomatic bag, and many of his correspondents sent the cost of return postage. His Christian friends, such as Charbonneau-Lassay and Olivier de Frémond, were concerned to know whether he was still a Christian and 'whether their efforts to save him were not sterile,' as de Frémond wrote in 1938.

The issue of Guénon's 'conversion' to Islam has long been a source of pain and misunderstanding to many. But for Guénon, conversion, as he wrote,

> has nothing in common with any exterior and contingent change, whether arising simply from the 'moral' domain.... Contrary to what takes place in 'conversion', nothing here implies the attribution of the superiority of one tradition form over another. It is merely a question of what one might call reasons of spiritual expediency, which is altogether different from simple individual preference....[1]

---

1. *Initiation and Spiritual Realization*, chap. 12.

Guénon had long been convinced, not that there was some kind of super-religion that would replace all existing religions, but that all religions enshrined primordial truth and were in essence saying the same thing. Doctrinal and dogmatic differences were at a lower level, that of the manifest created world of differences and divisions; all differences would be resolved as men sought the principial unity.

Occasionally news items appeared about him in the French press but they were mostly distortions and sometimes almost pure fiction. Perhaps the most authentic information about him can be derived from the articles he contributed regularly to *La Voile d'Isis* while refusing to accept the offer of some editorial responsibility. *La Voile d'Isis* continued publication until 1936 and was replaced by *Études Traditionnelles*. He also contributed occasional articles to Masonic periodicals, such as *The Speculative Mason,* and to the French periodical *Cahiers du Sud*. During his time in Egypt a number of Guénon's works were published. They were: *Symbolisme de la Croix* (1931); *Les États multiples de l'Être* (1932); *Règne de la Quantité et les Signes des Temps* (1945); *Principes du Calcul Infini-tésimal* (1946), a collection of his articles published between 1932 and 1938 under the title *Apercus sur l'Initiation,* and the last work published during his lifetime *La Grande Triad*.[2]

Guénon's life was that of a typical Egyptian bourgeois family, full of simple piety and gentle affection and sincerity. Nadjmoud Dine Bammate, an Afghan admirer, visited him after the war and gives us a charming and perceptive picture:

> The first impression one had of Guénon in his little bourgeois drawing-room in Cairo was, in spite of the Arab dress, which was in any case very simple, that of a French university Faculty member, a philosopher or an orientalist. A disconcerting im-pression since Guénon did not esteem either the one or the other. But in his elongated face, recalling Spaniards painted by El Greco, the eyes seemed to be out of place, added on, too large: they seemed

---

2. All but the fourth of these titles are currently available in English translation from Sophia Perennis, Hillsdale, NY. *The Metaphysical Principles of the Infinitesimal Calculus* is scheduled to appear soon.

to have some strange origin as if coming from another world, and in truth they were looking elsewhere.

From 1945 onwards Guénon suffered from a persistent cough, which wore him out and prevented him from working as much as he would have liked. In 1946 his wife made the pilgrimage to Mecca, in which he would like to have joined her but could not because he was not then an Egyptian citizen. In 1947 he received visits from Marco Pallis accompanied by A.K. Coomaraswamy's son. He had known the father previously and it was through him and Pallis, an expert on Buddhism and himself a Buddhist, that Guénon revised his ideas on Buddhism, which he had earlier dismissed as a Hindu heresy.

In 1950 his three children all fell ill at the same time and their father tended them, refusing all treatment for himself though he urgently needed it, since his legs were badly ulcerated. In January 1951 he grew rapidly worse: on the seventh of the same month the end came. Guénon knew he was dying and accepted it, calmly telling his wife that he wanted his workroom to be left untouched and that, although invisible, he would be 'there'. Late that evening he died.

The pilgrimage, which took a bright nervous little boy from Blois in the heart of France to Cairo, the ancient capital of one of the oldest civilizations in the world, and from Christianity to a belief in the transcendent unity of all religions, to use his friend Schuon's phrase, was over.

Only now, more than thirty years after his death, are we in the West beginning to catch up with his message. Some attempt to describe or relay that message is the subject matter of the second half of this book.

Cairo: Guénon at his work table, 1945

PART TWO

INTRODUCTION

THE WOUNDED AMAZON

IN CONFORMITY with Guénon's rooted mistrust of systematization in any shape or form, no attempt has been made in Part Two of this book to provide a systematic exposition of his thought. Instead, I have attempted to elucidate a number of themes which seem to me central for an understanding of Guénon's teaching.

What follows is a sequence of highly personal reflections on Guénon and his writings. Guénon does not provide a ready-made solution to life's problems or an infallible guide through the jungle of conflicting claims and ideologies; instead he directs our eyes to the farthest possible horizon of thought and demands imperiously that we stop at nothing less. With this most comprehensive outlook we can see all that is as an integrated whole, and so reverse the reign of quantity; in so doing, we can restore meaning and 'quality' to the manifest universe. This approach has resulted in a certain amount of repetition, which I have not attempted to eliminate because the ideas involved are many faceted and their reappearance in different contexts may help understanding.

If we are to attempt to understand Guénon's teaching as a whole, I think Mircea Eliade came somewhere near the truth when he wrote in his *Notebooks* (November 11, 1966):

> What Guénon and the other 'hermeticists' say of the tradition should not be understood on the level of historical reality (as they claim). These speculations constitute a universe of systematically articulated meanings: they are to be compared to a great poem or a novel. It is the same with Marxist or Freudian 'explanations'; they are true if they are considered as imaginary (potential) universes. The 'proofs' are few and uncertain—they

correspond to the historical, social, psychological 'realities' of a novel or poem.

All these global and systematic interpretations in reality constitute mythical creations, highly useful for understanding the world; but they are not, as their authors think, 'scientific explanations'.[1]

I have quoted this in full not only because I feel it contains an important element of truth, but because it also expresses certain commonly held misapprehensions about Guénon and his teaching. Firstly, the question of 'historical reality'. Guénon was often accused of being 'unhistorical', particularly in relation to his views on the origins of Masonic symbolism and teaching. It is true that he nowhere clearly states the historical 'evidence' for the date of the Templars' input into Freemasonry. For Guénon the fact that it is there is the significant point and the highly-charged emotional importance of the suppression of the Order and the martyrdom of Jacques de Molay give it a 'here and now' importance that can scarcely be denied. The fact that most Masons ignore or deride it is, in Guénon's view, no more than yet another example of degeneration in an initiatic order, as is seen also in the Catholic church and in Western society as a whole. The same applies to Rosicrucianism.

Guénon mistrusted the words 'system' and 'systematic', seeing in them the contingent element of limitation or restriction as opposed to the freedom of the comprehensive viewpoint. For him, the articulation of meanings as a whole is the outcome of intuition rather than reason; the facts have an inner coherence of their own and are organically linked at the level of imaginative intuition. The fundamental activity of the Divine Wisdom (*Hokmah*) is one of the free creative expressions of imagination, of which on earth the counterpart is the play of a child, or the cosmic dance of Shiva, and the outcome of which is not knowledge but joy.

The comparison of Guénon's exposition of the Advaita form of Vedanta with the body of Marxist or Freudian thought is highly misleading. Both Marx and Freud were deeply embedded in the

---

1. Mircea Eliade, *No Souvenirs. Journal 1957–1969* (NY, 1977), p291.

limitations and contingencies of nineteenth-century Europe and within those limitations built up their own individual systems—systems that bear their names today and are validated or invalidated by reference to their writings; writings that are those of an individual and are only very tenuously affiliated to any deeper and more permanent tradition. Guénon did not claim to have invented a new system of his own. He claimed—and rightly claimed—that he was merely the transmitter of a tradition as old as mankind and one quite distinct from the constructions of any single individual; the collective wisdom revealed from the beginning; the Logos, the *prisca theologia* of the early fathers. Recognition of this fundamental difference should prevent the emergence of 'Guénonians' and 'Guénonism', with all the odium, rancor, and exclusiveness that such movements invariably imply. For traditional wisdom has as its hallmark spontaneity, freshness, universality, and familiarity. The freedom that results from contact with the Ultimate Reality is analogous to the way of looking at life, with Clement of Alexandria, 'as a divine children's game.' Only the very simple and the very wise, the very young and the very experienced, can see it thus. The truly wise are those who can see things so clearly as to be able to understand their underlying unity, who can truly see heaven in a grain of sand and find all eternity in an hour. 'How can a wise man, knowing the unity of life, see all creatures in himself, be deluded or sorrowful?' (*Isha Upanishad*).

The *jñāna-yoga* or yoga of knowledge propounded by Guénon is the most difficult to grasp and to follow, and the least susceptible to formal discursive analysis or description. Consequently, it is the freest, most liberating, most personal, and the one that allows each follower to choose his own path. Whoever wishes to follow this path with Guénon must first accept the discipline of learning, the comprehension of the abstruse terminology, and the real intellectual effort involved in mastering the densely textured teaching. But the path is more direct and, for those who persevere and break through these barriers, there is a peace and certainty and, above all, joy in what Hippolitus of Rome calls 'the eternal feast of the Logos, the feast in which the Logos is the leader of the round-dance, as the dancing chorus of the earth returns to God.' The breakthrough from barrenness to the wonderful lightness and freedom of the cosmic dance—the free imaginative joy of intuitively joining in the great unity of all things—is what is being offered. But it is a state that can be attained only by renouncing all claims to it, all desire for it, and all intention of attaining it. It is truly a free unmerited gift of grace, spontaneously flowing from the source of our being.

Deliverance was Guénon's word for this state; freedom from all restriction and from all limitation, from all inhibiting individual and contingent states of being, and access to the fullest possible unity with the creative source of all, *deus ludens*.

> When we speak of God the creator playing, there lies concealed in that phrase the metaphysical truth that the creation of the world and of man, though a divinely meaningful act, was by no means a necessary one so far as God was concerned.[2]

At this level of concentration and commitment all intellectual speculation and rational discourse prove inadequate. What takes their place is joy in the never-ending wonder at the variety, perfection and infinite abundance of creation, moving and inter-relating in a cosmic harmony that we sense as being the totality of all things, as the consummation of all in the One. Words fail us; we do not need them now; we accept and rejoice that we are part of the cosmic dance and are not excluded.

> The sage is shy and humble,
> to the world he seems confusing.
> Men look at him and listen.
> He behaves like a little child.[3]

In every great religious tradition the child is the inheritor of the kingdom and the distinguishing characteristic of the child is that his actions are performed for the sheer joy of so acting—as play. In the end we aim at a like single-mindedness, a child-like concentration on the act, on the achievement of *une vérité vécue*, a truth lived spontaneously and fully; the serenity of the sage and the freedom of

---

2. Hugo Rahner, *Man at Play* (1964), p 11.
3. *Tao Te Ching*, chap. 49.

the man who feels at one with himself, his society, his environment, and with all that is; in short the state of feeling at home.

No easy task, and many fail to undertake it. One such was André Gide, who was familiar with Guénon's works and admired them. In his journal for October 1943 he writes about Guénon, and while admitting that he had greatly interested and influenced him, 'if only by reaction,' he says he is more than ever confirmed as a Westerner and as such wishes to retain his individuality and not be absorbed into the Eternal Being. This is a common misreading of the Vedantist idea of deliverance, which far from diminishing man's individuality, enhances it beyond all imagining. For in the final experience of union, or of the Beatific Vision, we, that is, our true selves, participate fully in the supreme fullness, so that far from being diminished or absorbed, our essential Self (*le Soi*) experiences the fullness of all its potentialities.

Henri Bosco describes a conversation with Gide during a later encounter in North Africa. Speaking of Guénon, Gide said, 'The bets have all been laid, I am too old now.' And Bosco adds, 'This turning again to himself so far from depressing him, comforted him.' And he went on:

> Anyhow, I love life passionately, life in all its multiplicity. I will not consent to allow my life to be deprived of the pleasure it derives from the marvelous diversity of the World. And for what? To sacrifice it to an abstraction, to Unity, an indefinable Unity! But definitions please me above all else. Only limited beings and perishable creatures are of interest to me and command my love, but not Being, limitless Being. I have no intention of losing myself in that. Quite the contrary, I intend to save myself from doing so, as long as I live.[4]

Most of us will want to say Amen to that, and Guénon would not condemn us, provided we see the ephemeral and contingent nature of this world and all that is in it and do not ignore the Ultimate Reality. I suspect that he might counsel those who feel like Gide to

---

4. René Guénon, *Les Dossier H*, ed. and arr. by *Pierre-Marie Sigaud* (Lausanne: L'Age d'Homme, 1984), pp 268 ff.

go ahead and exhaust all the possibilities of life in all its variety in order to reach that point of view where its underlying transience points us ineluctably towards its fulfillment in the perfection of its unchanging origin and destiny.

It cannot be emphasized too often that Guénon was no remote and abstract thinker living in an ivory tower, far removed from the concerns of the world as it is. In his writing, as a French academic with a mathematical background, he was strictly impersonal and avoided any trace of *sentimentalité*. But he was nevertheless passionately concerned with the fate of the West, his West, of which he was a part and for which he believed he had a message, to the delivery of which he devoted his life. In private he lived the life of a husband and a father, and acted as a caring and concerned guide to a host of correspondents. In all, he was a full human being who impressed many with his simple goodness and extraordinary patience and 'asceticism', though like his friend Coomaraswamy, he chain smoked. In his published work no traces of his personal life and character are found. In this one is reminded of the Amazons, who cut off their right breast in order not to impede their right arm when drawing the bow. There is something of this rigorous self-denial in Guénon also, and I find it admirable.

1

CLEARING THE GROUND

REASON AND BEYOND

THE MAGNITUDE of the task undertaken by Guénon in his virtually single-handed endeavor to turn Western thought in a fresh direction is almost impossible to grasp. For what he consciously or unconsciously was undertaking was the radical re-orientation of the prevailing trend of Western thought and its common mental outlook, deriving ultimately from Greek Aristotelian ways of thinking. Louis Rougier, in *La Métaphysique et le Langage,* has described the situation thus:

> For centuries Byzantines, Syrians, Jews, Arabs, and the Latin West learnt the same logical system, the same rudimentary ontology comprising 'the tree of Porphyry', that is, the ontological hierarchy of *species* and *genus,* the theory of categories, the theory of transcendentals, that of substance and accidence, form and matter; creating a common intellectual outlook which consisted of deducing the structure of reality from the analysis of language, discussing concepts instead of observing the facts of experience. They held as adequate the conceptual division which discursive thought imposes on things by explaining the world in terms of essences, predicate, substances and accidents.
> It is this common mental attitude which led to the belief in the existence of a universal reason and of its aptitude for elaborating a *philosophia perennis.*

Aristotle defined metaphysics as the science of 'being as being'; while other sciences study the different modes of Being, Ontology was the supreme science *ens est quod primum cadet in intellectu*. For Aristotle, and for long after him, metaphysics laid down the regulative principles for all other sciences. This emphasis on metaphysics as ontology, the Ultimate Reality, set the West on the path that was inevitably to lead it farther and farther away from the Principial Unity whose balance Aristotle upset when he discussed Being alone without the polar balance of Non-Being which Eastern philosophies have retained.

Louis Rougier traces this inclination back to certain special qualities of the Greek language which favored two tendencies inherent in Western thought and which even the most enlightened thinkers have difficulty in renouncing:

> 1. A spontaneous tendency towards nominal realism, that is to say, the belief that the word corresponds to the reality which it represents.

> 2. The tendency to conceptual realism, that is to say, discussing ready-made concepts rather than facts, i.e. accepting as an adequate description of reality the conceptual division which discursive thought imposes on the data of the senses.

The dependence of thought on language is typically Greek and so now Western also, and is opposed to Eastern thought, which starts from the deep conviction that 'the Tao that can be told is not the Eternal Tao.' This elevation of discussion and argument coincided with the appearance of democracy and the growing importance of being able to use the spoken word to persuade the masses, as exemplified by the rise of oratory. Athenian society must have been one of the most talkative in the world and we in the West have been talking ever since. It is worth pointing out in this connection the etymologies of the words 'discuss' and 'argue'; the former comes from the Latin *discutere*, 'to strike asunder, dash to pieces, shatter', and the latter from the root *arg*, meaning 'clear, shining, visible'. There are here already signs of an incipient scientific materialism that maintains that the way to grasp reality is to break it up into pieces, and that what cannot be seen or otherwise apprehended by the senses does not exist with the same reality of being that the phenomenal world, including man, possesses.

Guénon's message was to deny this one-sided approach by concentrating on a special form of Hindu thought, the Advaita Vedanta. In order to follow him in this, we have from the outset to adopt a different procedure to the one we usually employ. Dionysius the Areopagite wrote that when you work on a text, that is study; but when you let the text work on you, that is *lectio*. This, as it were, passive approach is needed to apprehend the Principal Unity whose full truth is only revealed as Ruysbroeck says when 'the powers of the mind are simplified above reason.' Western man has tended to reject the infinite out of fear of the unknown and as a result has failed to understand, because he has made ultimate his own finiteness. Or as Coleridge put it in his *Biographia Literaria:*

> A system, the first principle of which is to render the mind intuitive of the spiritual in man (i.e., of that which lies on the other side of our natural consciousness) must needs have a great obscurity for those who have never disciplined and strengthened this ulterior consciousness.

This ulterior consciousness was what Guénon meant when he said that the Ultimate Principal Unity can only be apprehended by 'direct intellectual intuition'.

We must be careful at the outset not to confuse Guénon's use of the words 'intellect' and 'intellectual' with Cartesian notions of reason and rationality. His understanding is far closer to that of the medieval schoolmen. In this context it becomes clear why Guénon was unable to conform to the neo-Thomism of his friend Maritain. A full discussion of the age-old problem of the limits of the intellect and its relation to the senses is beyond the scope of this work. But, as elsewhere in Guénon's writings, great care is needed in finding what he meant by the words he uses, which is often far from current usage.

For Guénon, the discovery of Hindu thought was a marvelous liberation from the confusion of modern Western thought where everything seems to be obscured by subjective individualism, the cult of personality, and a complete lack of any conception of the existence of a Principial Reality. It was this principle and the truths that stem from it that Guénon found in Hindu thought. If we are to follow him we must endeavor to free ourselves from all post-Aristotelian Western ideas and travel East.

Our journey will take us to the Indian sub-continent and the Aryan nation whose wonderful collection of poetic chants and prayers known as the Vedas are the basis of their civilization.

Their origins are untraceable, but some time between 1400 and 1200 BC they were collected, and it is this collection which is still held in reverence by millions of Hindus.

Sanskrit, the language in which they were composed, is simple, regular, and unambiguous and has a very copious vocabulary. Its lexical content is based on three thousand monosyllabic roots, each having a definite, almost physical meaning. New compounds can be formed at will, and in them the basic meanings of the syllables are preserved (words of up to fifty syllables are not unknown). In Sanskrit the range of spoken sounds has almost the regularity of a musical scale. It is a wonderful instrument for poetic utterance, the words themselves giving rise directly to images; no language is better suited to the description of nature. It is indeed the *surabani* or 'language of the Gods' of which the *devangari* or divine scripture is composed. As Greek and Hebrew have molded the ideas of the West and given them their particular shape, so has Sanskrit shaped the expression of Hindu thought.

These sacred hymns are the texts on which Vedanta, which means 'the end of the Vedas', is based, by way of commentary. These commentaries immediately present Western readers with a problem since they comprise both a system of thought and scriptural exegesis. They remind us that Hindu thought is neither theological nor philosophical in the separate Western senses of those words, but unites elements of both and is aimed at providing a practical guide to spiritual experience. Such a position, or something akin to it, was formerly the case in the West at the time when theology was considered to be the queen of the sciences, the uniting force relating and crowning all other knowledge. But Hindu thought has never made a separation between philosophy and theology and has retained a unity which the divisive analytical spirit of the West finds hard to accept. Guénon was not interested in the historical influences that molded the evolution of Hindu thought over the centuries; he was content to expound the Advaita form of Vedan-tism of Shankara as he had learnt it.

In Hindu thought the unifying principle that keeps all the various parts together is the concept of *Brahma*, the Ultimate Reality or Principal Unity, as Guénon often called it. Brahma is the subject matter of all Indian thought, which is not speculative so much as practical, the aim being to provide mankind with the means of deliverance by union with this Principal Unity. Through the centuries six different ways of approaching the study of this Ultimate Reality have evolved. They are known as the six *Darshanas* or insights, which may with some reservations be compared to schools of philosophical thought. But as Guénon points out, they are complementary and not contradictory. Furthermore, though they bear the name of an individual, they are not the personal views of one man but the expression of a collective view held by many and are an example of distinction as opposed to division.

Vedanta is the most widely known and studied of the six *Darshanas*. Within its study three main schools of thought have arisen, associated with the names of their putative founders, Shankara, Ramanuja, and Madhva. Shankara was the great proponent of *Advaita*, which in Sanskrit means non-dualism. It is the most completely apophatic (negative) of all the schools and follows the Western *via negativa* most closely. A study of Shankara's commentaries and Guénon's interpretations of them in his two early books *Introduction to the Study of the Hindu Doctrines* (1921) and *Man and His Becoming according to the Vedānta* (1925) is the essential basis for an understanding of all Guénon's other ideas.[1] For when, as he frequently does, he refers to metaphysical thought, he does not mean any Western interpretation of that term, but rather the Advaitan interpretation of the Vedanta.

All begins and ends with *Brahma*, the Principal Unity, which is beyond all conception and only recognizable as the experience of

---

1. See also *Studies in Hinduism*. ED.

saccindananda, i.e., 'being' (*sac*), 'consciousness' (*cit*), and 'bliss' (*ananda*). Nothing can be said about *Brahma*, for speech is a function of the world of manifestation, so whatever can be said must therefore be partial and inadequate. The only way *Brahma* can be known is through the experience of direct intellectual intuition. This experience can be achieved by means of strict discipline with the aim of acquiring understanding. This discipline is one of the various *yogas* or paths to *moksa* or deliverance. The particular yoga connected with Advaita Vedanta is *jñāna-yoga*, the discipline of knowledge.

In his excellent book on *Advaita Vedanta* Professor Eliot Deutsch, to whom I am much indebted, outlines the four qualifications that must be fulfilled by the person who would attain *moksa* and the three stages he must complete in order to do so. The four qualifications are in brief. (1) the possession of the natural ability to discern between reality and illusion, i.e., discrimination (*viveka*); (2) readiness to give up all sensuous pleasures and distractions and become indifferent to them, as also to all desire to enjoy the fruits of one's actions here or hereafter (*vairagya*); (3) the practice of mental tranquillity, self-control, dispassion, endurance, concentration, and faith, all of which is collectively known as *satsampat*; (4) right desire (*mumuksatva*), that is to say, desire for deliverance above anything else.

The three stages are first, hearing (*sravan*); second, discriminating understanding (*manana*); and thirdly, constant meditation and awareness (*nididhyasana*).

If we follow this extremely challenging path we shall learn to view Brahma firstly as the Ultimate Ineffable Reality (*nirguna Brahman*), and secondly, from within our limitations, as the *Brahman* to which we can ascribe qualities (*saguna Brahman*). The first might be compared with the *hypertheousios* of Dionysius the Areopagite, or the *Gottheit* of Eckhart, and the latter with the God of conventional theology, though Guénon always warned against the too facile equating of concepts in Eastern thought with others in the West. Nevertheless, as Guénon frequently pointed out, the West also once shared in the knowledge of the Primordial Tradition and throughout the centuries traces of it can still be found.

As Professor Deutsch says:

> The *sadhana catustaya* or fourfold discipline of Vedanta is clearly not one that any merely rational person can follow. It requires a radical change in the natural direction of consciousness, leading one to a dispassionate involvement with the things of the world. Advaita Vedanta is explicitly aristocratic in its contention that, practically speaking, truth or genuine knowledge is available only to the few who, by natural temperament and disposition, are willing and able to undertake all the arduous demands that its quest entails.

This considered opinion of a great Western student of Advaita Vedanta underlines two things that have puzzled some people about Guénon. Firstly, although he was completely detached in his writings, he was passionately concerned with the fate of the West. Secondly, he believed implicitly that the restoration of traditional wisdom could only be carried out through the patient building up of an 'elite' who would collaborate with Eastern thinkers in the restoration of authentic traditional ways of life and thought.

Guénon was very conscious that the message he felt called upon to transmit was not easily to be understood. In *The Spiritist Fallacy* (1923) he wrote:

> Doubtless it will be further charged that the arguments we have expounded are too difficult to grasp, that they have the drawback of not being within everyone's compass. This may be true in some measure, even though we have always tried to be as clear as possible. But we are not among those who believe it well to conceal certain difficulties or to simplify things to the detriment of the truth.[2]

Even those who had devoted a long time to the study of Guénon's writings found them difficult. François Ménard, an old friend and admirer and a founding member of the Masonic Lodge *The Great Triad*, was a case in point. In a letter to a friend written in 1946 and quoted in Paul Chacornac's *The Simple Life of René Guénon* he said: 'Guénon's books demonstrate that particular confusion which does

---

2. *The Spiritist Fallacy*, pt2, chap. 14

not exclude clear-sightedness or clear expression, but yet results in one's being quite unable to extract any precise ideas from them.' I think this has also been the experience of many other readers of Guénon and is, I believe, indicative of the way in which we approach ideas that are new to us. We are inclined to see them as the personal opinion of the author and we attempt to determine whether he is on our side or against us. Subtly and without admitting it, we are looking always for confirmation or at best enlargement of views we already hold. Something as impersonal and uncompromisingly foreign as the message relayed by Guénon disturbs us and at first we are inclined to resist it as we would resist the presumptuous opinions of any other individual. But Guénon's work, as he repeatedly said, is not the personal opinion of himself or anyone else. It is the collective wisdom of the Vedanta as viewed by the Advaita School and as such is no more personal—perhaps rather less so—than the propositions of Euclid, or the steps of any other mathematical proof.

All in the end (or in the beginning) stems from the Principial Unity or Ultimate Reality, which, while being the final reference point of all that is said, is yet a reality beyond the grasp of reason or discursive thought. Guénon's work is impregnated with this basic contradiction. It is worth recalling here, I think, that in the East all transmission of knowledge was performed orally with the help of a *guru* or master. Hearing and seeing one who has himself mastered the teaching and transmits it, is, surprisingly perhaps, less personal than reading the same thing in a book, because in reading we have no supporting evidence beyond the words themselves, whereas in front of a teacher we have the evidence of all our senses as to the authenticity of his claim to be nothing more than the means of transmission of a collective wisdom that is not solely concerned with him as a person. Anyone who has received such teaching from an authentic teacher of this kind will immediately know what is being referred to.

Speaking of the teaching given by Krishna and Arjuna in the *Ātmā-Gītā*, Guénon said that

> from the interior point of view, the teaching given by Krishna and Arjuna is that of supra-rational intellectual intuition, whereby the 'Self' communicates with the 'ego' when the latter is

'qualified' and prepared in such a way that this communication can be effectively established.³

In other words, in all effective teaching it is the Atman who is the teacher, and the master merely the transmitter of the message. It can, I think, be understood in another way, as what the French call *une verité vécue,* a lived truth, reminding us of the words of Dionysius quoted earlier in this chapter, and also of some words of Simone Weil:

> It is not enough to have perceived [a given truth], given it one's attention, understood it; it must be given a permanent place in the mind, so that it may be present even when one's attention is directed towards something else.

For over a hundred years now the West has been besotted by the cult of the individual, his own separate importance, his own individual consciousness, his own inner life, his personal salvation. Our thought has been dominated by individualism and immanence. Man has increasingly felt that all is to be found in himself, by himself, in the exercise of his reason, and for himself. Guénon's message helps to restore the balance by pointing to the pole of transcendence and our ultimate dependence on the unknowable, ineffable and transcendent reality, *Brahma.*

Guénon was—not unexpectedly—opposed to all forms of modern depth psychology and went to considerable lengths to propose an entirely different conception of the human being:

> Human individuality is at once much more and much less than Westerners generally suppose it to be: much more, because they recognize in it scarcely anything except the corporeal modality, which includes but the smallest fraction of its possibilities; much less, however, because this individuality, far from really constituting the whole being, is but one state of that being among an indefinite multitude of other states.⁴

---

3. *Studies in Hinduism,* chap. 1.
4. *Man and His Becoming according to the Vedānta,* chap. 2.

Guénon made a clear distinction between *le soi* (the self) and *le moi* (the ego), the former being eternal and the latter being a contingent part of the world of manifestation. His opposition to depth psychology was at least in part based on his conviction that this distinction was not clearly sustained. The 'profane' search within for personal salvation and union with the immanent deity was for Guénon a travesty of authentic Vedanta teaching. Vedanta has always maintained that it is impossible to reach the higher by means of the lower: the reverse is the only possible way. The higher illuminates and clarifies the nature of the lower, which, thus prepared, can achieve that unity with the Ultimate Principle which is called Deliverance, deliverance from the illusion of the separate ego.

Jivātmā, the living soul, due to its origin in the realm of manifestation, suffers from the illusion that it is separated from the *Atman*, which is its true ground. It is distinct from it, but not separate from it. Such distinctions without separation are difficult for the modern Western mind to encompass, as they are not compatible with rational thought, which insists that things must be either this or that and balks at the suggestion that they are in fact both this and that, summed up in the Sanskrit phrase *tat tvam asi*, thou art that.

The process for Westerners of recovering what they once knew will be slow, since, as we have suggested, it requires a commitment that goes far beyond intellectual assent and demands a *metanoia* or change of mind. It is this change that Guénon realizes is the crux of the matter, since it means for each one who attempts it a radical reorientation of his thought, including his attitude towards himself as an individual of infinite worth. Guénon urges us to great humility when he points out that 'from the purely metaphysical point of view ... the case of man can never appear as a privileged one.' Having said this, we must also remind ourselves that Vedanta takes man and his potentialities and actual condition very seriously and that Guénon was concerned throughout his life with 'the nature and constitution of the human being.'

This concern would lead many Western readers to expect Guénon to refer to modern anthropological, psychological, and sociological notions. But he warns us at the very beginning that:

Genuine knowledge ... has little if anything to do with 'profane' knowledge. The studies which go to make up the latter cannot be looked upon even as an indirect path of approach to the 'Sacred Sciences'; on the contrary, at times they even constitute an obstacle by reason of the often incurable deformation which is the commonest consequence of a certain kind of education.

Obviously, what is required of us is far more than the mere intellectual effort required to master an abstruse treatise on any subject, and Guénon was aware that 'many are called and few chosen.' We cannot ourselves determine our status; we can simply make the effort.

Guénon has naturally enough been accused of preaching a new religion and some may draw back for fear that their religious faith will be weakened. This question will be dealt with at length later on; here it is sufficient to say that metaphysics in the Vedantist meaning of the word is the basis on which all true religion must be built and has nothing to do with the doctrines or dogmas of the various religions as we know them today.

2

CROSSING THE MEDITERRANEAN

THE ENCOUNTER OF EAST AND WEST

IN THE CHAPTER called 'The Classical Prejudice' in his *Introduction to the Study of the Hindu Doctrines* Guénon says:

> Westerners, because their own civilization does not date back much beyond the Greco-Roman era and is almost entirely derived from it, are inclined to believe that it must have been the same everywhere, and they have difficulty in conceiving of very different civilizations whose origins are much older than their own; one might say that intellectually they are incapable of crossing the Mediterranean.

The belief that Western civilization is the highest and most successful embodiment of legitimate human aspirations is still maintained, although with increasing doubt and difficulty, by most people in the West, though not substantially anywhere else.

We eagerly concentrate our hopes on any passing phenomena that seem to support this belief. Japanese and Chinese musicians interpreting Beethoven and Mozart, Indian writers publishing successful novels, Africans writing poetry in French; all these and many other signs are taken to indicate that a coming World Civilization is peacefully on its way. The Yankee enthusiasm of a Buckminster Fuller and the McLuhan concept of the global village are all seized upon and exploited to reinforce the idea that the West will remain powerful and continue to dominate by means of its technological superiority and the entrepreneurial skills of the multi-national corporations. But the contra-indications cannot and will not be ignored. The ever-present threat of atomic war, the squandering of world resources, the ever-increasing strain which the world monetary system is placing on the developing nations—these and the collapse of moral, ethical and social restraints keep us uneasy with, and critical of, ourselves without pointing to any way of improving the situation. Dr Alfred Métraux summed up the problem thirty years or more ago when he wrote in the *UNESCO Courier*:

> Racism is one of the most disturbing manifestations in the vast revolution taking place in the world. Just at the moment when our industrial civilization is penetrating every part of the world, uprooting men of every kind from their most ancient traditions, a pseudo-scientific doctrine is invoked to justify to these same people, deprived of their cultural heritage, the denial to them of any real participation in the benefits of civilization which we are imposing on them. So at the very center of our civilization we find a contradiction. On the one hand the West hopes for and indeed demands the assimilation of other cultures to its own values, to which it attributes a perfection which it will not allow to be criticized, and on the other hand it cannot bring itself to admit that two-thirds of humanity outside the West are capable of reaching objectives we propose to them. By a strange irony the most grievously wounded victims of this racial dogmatism are precisely those individuals who by their natural intelligence or education, demonstrate its falsity.[1]

A different angle on the same situation is presented by Professor Jean Servier, an ethnologist, in his book *L'Homme et l'Invisible* (1980) in which he destroys convincingly the white man's myth of evolutionary progress summed up in the phrase 'from ape-man to astronaut', a phrase implying that primitive man is the fossil witness to an evolutionary process culminating in white Western civilization, mankind's highest achievement so far. Such a point of view,

---

1. *Unesco Courier*, vol. 3, nos. 6–7 (1950).

Professor Servier maintains, is both contradicted by the facts and is a willful act of wishful thinking. He continues by pointing out that the defining characteristic of man at all times and in all places is his unshakable contact with and recognition of what might be called the numinous, the sacred, or as he himself prefers to call it, the Invisible.

I think that this comprehensive context, which embraces the whole of human history and the entire terrestrial globe, is the right setting in which to consider Guénon's attacks on the modern Western mentality and his profound interest in and admiration for the East. East and West are not primarily geographical or even cultural distinctions; they are symbols of two different fundamental attitudes towards reality. The West, especially during the last 500 years, but essentially throughout its history of some 2,000 years, has concentrated the greater part of its attention on the phenomenal world of matter, and has lost touch with the suprasensible reality which Servier calls *l'Invisible*. The East, on the other hand, has concentrated on the transcendent reality accessible only to man by direct intellectual intuition. The West has followed the path into the depths of matter, the East has traditionally followed the path into the heights of spirit or immateriality. Both have dealt with the neglected aspect of the whole in their different ways. The West has separated spirit from matter, and created categories which do not exist in the East, notably separation between sacred and secular, between God and Man, between heaven and earth, between mind and matter, body and spirit. None of these divisions is taken as valid in the traditional East. In the East they have retained in a remarkable way a unity, with distinctions within that unity, but no divisions which destroy the unity.

Since science and the penetration of matter depend on division, separation and analysis and the pursuit of 'either/or', the West has penetrated matter and the material world and gained mastery over it. In so doing people have become convinced that matter, over which they have gained such mastery, is the only reality, to the extent that even energy is now considered as 'matter'. This attitude has rendered man unaware of his true place in the scheme of things. It has encouraged in him delusions of grandeur, of supremacy, of omnipotence, all of which are patently, even to Western man himself when he stops to think, untrue and inconsistent with the reality of his nature and status in the cosmos.

The East has until recently avoided this restless activity spurred on by curiosity, which has opened the Pandora's box of nature and let loose forces, powers and potentialities which man is incapable of using wisely. In our arrogance we despise the East for its 'inertia', for its preference for being rather than doing. We find the Chinese concept of *wu-wu-wei*, 'activate inactivity', meaningless and vaguely threatening. A personal experience may perhaps illuminate the difference. A friend attended a conference of philosophers in India where the metaphysics of the Vedanta were being discussed and expressions of the superiority of Eastern over Western thought were being aired. My friend, exasperated, asked them what was the use of all this theorizing; were they really so very much better off than the West? At least there were not hundreds of dying people to be found on the pavements of London or New York!

Such a response is both futile and unconsciously arrogant. I do not know if my friend's Indian hosts thought of Hiroshima or Auschwitz, but they could be forgiven if they did so. Was it not Mother Teresa herself who pointed out that the spiritual poverty of the West was infinitely worse than the material poverty of the East?

I think it would not be altogether unfair to suggest that the attitude of many Westerners today when confronted with the East is that of a callow self-assertive adolescent when confronted with the patience and tolerance of someone older and more experienced than himself. Rabindranath Tagore, in his autobiography, confesses that much as he admired European literature, he had to admit that he found it, even Shakespeare, rather immature.

Guénon's personal disillusionment with the West began very early and was fuelled by his early contacts with Islam and with Taoist thought as taught him by Matgioi, who also added a strong tinge of anti-Christian teaching as well. The emptiness of all esoteric depth in the Church's official teaching and its sterile sentimentality also contributed to Guénon's rejection of it.

In his very first book, *Introduction to the Study of the Hindu Doctrines* (1921), Guénon devotes many pages to a scathing critique of the way in which Western students of the East have misinterpreted Hindu doctrines. There is no doubt that his general disillusionment with the occult establishment of his time was another important factor. He had entered that world hoping, if not actually believing, that somewhere within it he would find an authentic expression of the Western version of the Primordial Tradition, so clearly to be found in Eastern teaching; but he was bitterly disappointed.

His disappointment was expressed in his next two books. *Theosophy: History of a Pseudo-Religion,* also published in 1921, was part of a series edited by his friend Jacques Maritain. In it he combines disgust with the general attitude of Western scholars to the East with a disgust at the way in which the most widely known occult organization had revealed itself to be a mere farrago of misunderstood Eastern teaching and Western occult ideas. He was as critical of Theosophy's co-founder, Madame Blavatsky, as he was later about G.I. Gurdjieff. In Guénon's view, nothing good could come from any such amalgams of ignorance, sentimentality, and deliberate duplicity.

In his next book, *The Spiritist Fallacy* (1923), he had even more opportunity to express his near despair at the propagation of what he calls *contre-verités* or counter-truths. He writes a lot about the moral and psychological harm which has been done to many adherents of spiritualism. Very early on he states that Spiritualism's fundamental tenet, communication with the spirits of the dead, 'is an impossibility pure and simple.'

Guénon's teaching often takes the form of an exposition of error. For instance, in critiquing Spiritualism he rightly claims that it adopts the Cartesian dualism of mind and body instead of the traditional tripartite division into body, mind and spirit. In traditional teaching, body and mind are both part of the realm of manifestation and thus relative and contingent: even though the mind has a subtle corporeity, it does not and cannot have any part in the spirit or true vital principle which is alone the true person, permanent and imperishable. Communication with this spirit through mediums after death is utterly impossible. He points out that in traditional societies mediums are considered mentally ill. He does not deny the reality of psychic phenomena such as table-rapping, telekinesis and even materialization, bilocation and other related phenomena, but he believes they all fall within the realm of the mind and are thus strictly part of the world of manifestation and not the spiritual world. He also points out how Spiritualism and Theosophy indulge in what he calls transposed materialism and, what is more, have close links with certain left-wing political elements.

One other aspect of Guénon's teaching which many have found puzzling is his belief in what has been called the 'conspiracy theory' of history. Writing about the rise of the Spiritualist movements, for instance, he suggests that 'adepts' provoked the Spiritualist movement for their own purposes. Psychic phenomena, he noted, have occurred before without giving rise to any such widespread popular movement. He suggests that the 'adepts' may have been members of the Hermetic Brotherhood of Luxor, who acted by means of a sort of suggestion on the inhabitants and visitors to Hydesville, the home town of the Fox sisters, founders of modern Spiritualism (*The Spiritist Fallacy*, pt 1, chap. 2). He concludes by stating quite categorically: 'We do not believe in spontaneous movements, either religious or political, or in the dubious realm in which we are now.'

One of the doctrines shared by Spiritualism and Theosophy—a doctrine widely believed in the West to be orthodox Hindu belief—is that of reincarnation. According to Guénon the possibility of such an event is strictly contrary to traditional teaching and the widespread belief in it in theosophical and spiritualist circles, and even in Christian circles, is due to a fundamental misunderstanding of Hindu teaching. The journey of the soul is acceptable, but the conception of a return to another corporeal envelope and a repetition of a stage already passed through is to apply purely Western interpretations to the word 'body', for instance, which are not at all what is meant by the Sanskrit word so translated.

I do not think it necessary to elaborate on all that Guénon found wrong with the modern world as set out in the three books *Introduction to the Study of the Hindu Doctrines*, *East and West*, and *The Crisis of the Modern World*, all of which have been translated into English. It is important, though, to consider Guénon's rela-tionship with Islam, the exoteric forms of which he eventually adopted as his own choice of religious allegiance.

As we have seen, his contacts with Islam began early in his life when he was initiated into a Muslim *ṭarīqah*, which normally would have involved adherence to Muslim rites and ceremonies, but the doctrine of *taqīyah* or *resenatio mentalis*, common in Shī'ah Islam, may have enabled him to carry on as a Christian exoterically while in his heart he felt himself to be a Muslim, a variety of 'conversion' commoner than is sometimes believed. Some quotations from *East and West* may help elucidate this matter when he writes that 'all traditional doctrines are identical in essence' and 'theological truths may be considered an adaptation of certain metaphysical truths to a special point of view'; and again, 'metaphysics and religion are not, and never will be, on the same plane. It follows furthermore that a purely metaphysical doctrine and a religious doctrine cannot enter into rivalry or conflict, since their domains are clearly different.'

Guénon, in answering queries as to why he had been converted to Islam, replied that it was not a question of conversion but rather one of spiritual economy, by which he meant, I believe, that for him the ultimate truth was metaphysical and that religious truths were, as he said, adaptations of metaphysical truths. Guénon was not by nature inclined to involvement at the level of emotion or sentiment in religious beliefs. He frequently condemned Christianity for *sentimentalité*, a word which in French has a wider and less pejorative meaning than it has in English and includes much of what we would call emotion.

Islam for Guénon was both temperamentally attractive in its simplicity and unity and practically convenient in that it was the religion of the country in which he chose to spend much of his life. There is one further and perhaps much more decisive reason why Guénon adopted Islam as his expression of faith in the exoteric sphere. His contact with Islam had always been with teaching derived from the *Shaykh al-Akbar*, better known in the West as Ibn Arabi, who was the reopener of the initiatic way in Islam in the seventh century of the Hegira. As Michel Valsan, himself a Muslim, remarks:

> René Guénon's teaching and that of Ibn Arabi share more than a simple concordance between two true metaphysicians. There is

also a subtle relationship, and a more direct one, in that René Guénon received his Islamic initiation at the hands of a master who had himself been nourished by the intellectual power and spirit of the Shaykh al-Akbar: I mean the Egyptian Shaykh 'Ilaysh al-Kabir....[2]

Valsan points out that:

> The Islamic doctrine is formal on the point that all the divine Messengers have brought essentially the same message and that all the Traditions are in essence one.... As regards the Islamic form of the tradition, this is in any case originally and essentially based on the doctrine of Supreme Identity, which is that of the *waḥdat al-wujūd,* an expression coined by the Shaykh al-Akbar but expressing a truly Islamic concept ... which the master only rendered fully explicit and more comprehensible to contemporary intellectuals![3]

But it should be remembered that although Guénon himself adopted Islam, he was firmly opposed to proselytism of any kind. For him the truly religious man of the future would seek to hold fast to the universally accepted metaphysical truths and to live by them in whatever religious community he found, either from upbringing or conscious decision, to be most congenial. In so doing he would endeavor to include insights and points of view, and even some forms of worship, from other religious traditions, so that his own formulation might be enriched by inclusion and not impoverished by an exclusive refusal to accept new elements of true spirituality. This is what I think Guénon meant when he spoke of 'a secondary assimilation' (*une assimilation au second degré*). Certain enlightened and thus open-hearted people would be influenced, as many have been already, by Eastern thought and would thereby find greater truth and depth in their own formulae, which without such a new infusion are always in danger of becoming sterile.

---

2. M. Valsan, *L'Islam et la Fonction de René Guénon* (Paris, 1984), p 30.
3. Valsan, loc. cit., p 14.

People who adopt this point of view will form an élite group, about which Guénon wrote so much and which has puzzled so many of his readers. The translators of his works into English have avoided using the word élite and chosen the less definite word 'elect'. But élite, meaning, as the *OED* says, 'the choice part, the best', is what Guénon meant. He envisaged a number of enlightened people, many of whom might be in some way connected with the Church, who would strive to live according to the Primordial Tradition and to share it with other like-minded people. No formal organization with rules and regulations would be appropriate. Perhaps something similar to the Aquarian conspiracy as envisaged by Marilyn Ferguson was what he had in mind. But it must be remembered that Guénon, like all true traditional thinkers, did not believe in the rule of *demos*, and realized the futility of trying to make the doctrines relating to the Primordial Tradition easily available to everyone:

> We spoke just now of 'popularization'. This is another thing altogether peculiar to modern civilization, and in it may be seen one of the chief factors of this state of mind that we are trying to describe. It is one of the forms taken by this strange need for propaganda which animates the Western mind, and which can only be explained by the predominant influence of sentiment. No intellectual consideration justifies proselytism, in which the Easterners see nothing but a proof of ignorance and incomprehension.... Popularization necessarily involves... the debasement of all knowledge to the level of the limited understanding of the masses.[4]

Such ideas can never be popular in the present climate of public opinion and they certainly lay those who hold them open to the charge of arrogance; but deep down most people know that a hierarchical structuring of society is more likely to produce stability and mutual respect and a sense of duty than is our present demented attempt to achieve universal equality in all things.

One of the Hindu concepts to which Guénon not infrequently refers is that of caste, a system which appears utterly abhorrent to a

---

4. Guénon, *East and West*, chap. 2.

modern Western Christian democrat. A strong case may well be made out for saying that in its present form it condemns large numbers of people to the performance of necessary but 'degrading' functions. But who has told them that their functions are degrading? Gandhi, the great Hindu leader, did not. He believed that all necessary activities are honorable and should be performed by all. If a certain pharisaism has crept into the system, this is an obvious and urgent reason for reforming the system, not for destroying it. Speaking of the religious attitudes of the Indo-Europeans, Professor H. Günther wrote:

> The caste law is regarded as corresponding to the law of the world order (*dharma*) or the *ius divinum* of the Romans. Participation in the superior spiritual world of the Vedas, Brahmanas and Upanishads, originally determined the degree of caste. The higher the caste the stricter the sense of duty to lead a life corresponding to the World Order.[5]

The endeavor to find valid alternatives to the present state of the West is a challenging and difficult task. Guénon dealt mainly in the most comprehensive principles and seldom made specific suggestions as to possible immediate action. With regard to the formation of an elite, he did suggest that it might be possible for people sufficiently interested in his writings to get together in study groups. This has been implemented with varying results. The formation of a Masonic lodge, *La Grande Triade,* was a failure, while the international colloquium at Cerisy-la-Salle in 1973 was a success, as the volume of reports of the speeches and discussions amply proves.[6] It is to be hoped that such a gathering for English-speaking students of Guénon may one day be called, perhaps under the auspices of the Ibn Arabi Society, whose efforts to promote an authentic traditional teaching are much to be respected.

For the time being we wait expectantly, as we draw near to the end of the *Kali-Yuga*, or dark age, so graphically described in the

---

5. H. Günther, *Religious Attitudes of the Indo-Europeans* (1977), p 49.
6. *René Guénon et l'atualité de la Pensée traditionnelle.* Actes du Colloque Internationale de Cerisy-la-Salle, July 13–20, 1973 (Milan, 1980).

Vishnu Purana:

> Races of slaves will become masters of the world.
> Leaders will be by nature violent.
> Leaders instead of protecting their subjects will despoil them.
> The only union between the sexes will be that of pleasure.
> The earth will only be appreciated for its mineral wealth.
> Life will become uniform at the heart of a universal promiscuity.
> He who hands out most money will dominate men.
> Every man will imagine himself to be the equal
> of a spiritual authority.
> Folk will fear death and the thought of poverty will appall them.
> Women will become no more than sexual playthings.

Those who have raised their eyes above the all-enveloping fog will be quietly preparing the ground for the new age which will begin at that mysterious moment outside time and space when the change takes place.

Optimism and pessimism are equally irrelevant. Guénon said that his work 'had nothing to do with pessimism,' but he also rightly said 'the Truth does not have to be consoling.'

The attitude of the Taoist sage sums up our task:

> The sage goes about doing nothing, teaching no-talking.
> The ten thousand things rise and fall without cease,
> Creating yet not possessing
> Working yet not taking credit
> Work is done, then forgotten.
> Therefore it lasts for ever.[7]

---

7. *Tao Te Ching,* chap. 2.

3

THE VOICE BEHIND THE FAN

TRADITION AND SOCIETY

TRADITION as understood by Guénon has certain con-comitants which are repugnant to the West as a whole but which here and there throughout the centuries have been recognized as essential to the happiness and stability of society.

We have already commented on the idea of novelty and originality so very much prized by modern Westerners. Few realize that this concept is scarcely more than two hundred years old. Fewer still realize, as Guénon did, how false, and consequently harmful, it is. One of those who did was Archbishop William Temple, who some fifty years ago wrote:

> The modern world, with its strange, new and probably transient belief in 'progress', tends to give much credit to 'originality' even to the point of doubting whether anything else is quite sincere. It wants a new contribution to thought, and in its grotesque individualism supposes that every man who truly expresses his own relation to the world, will say something different from what anyone else would say. But there must be some great and fundamental truths in comparison with which the peculiar reactions of individual souls are an irrelevance and an impertinence, and of which a man should seek to be no more than an undistorting medium. (*Readings in St John's Gospel,* p120)

These great and fundamental truths are the subject matter of what is 'handed on' in tradition, and Guénon would certainly have agreed with Temple that in handing them on, man 'should seek to be no more than an undistorting medium'. Indeed, in conversation with his Afghan friend Nadjmoud-Dine Bammate, who visited him in Cairo towards the end of his life, Guénon spoke about himself as a teacher in these terms:

> It is not a question of being persuasive, still less of beguiling, but simply of stating what is, without any addition of one's own inclinations or learning, nor of one's intellectual cleverness, and without the intrusion of any external matter. One thinks of *recto tono* reading in the Buddhist tradition, which recommends spiritual masters to convey their teaching in a neutral almost colorless voice, the timbre unchanging and verging on the monotonous. If the level of delivery is broken by some inflection, the learner's attention is in danger of being distracted. The master should be careful never to thrust himself forward in the discourse. It is for this reason that for greater safety the speaker should hide his face behind a fan. For acceptance is to be given to truth alone, not to any false glamour of eloquence or traces of personality.

One sees here at once a profound difference between East and West. In India the function of the highest caste, that of the Brahman, was to preserve and pass on the traditional wisdom, for the maintenance of the whole social order depended on this being done in the proper way so that continuity and stability might be secured. This explains the enormous reverence accorded to the sage, the *guru* and the shaykh or *pir* in Eastern societies. In China the situation was slightly different in that more emphasis was laid on the social outcome of the teaching and the solidarity of the nation; ancestors were reverenced (but not worshipped) as those who were the guardians of the tradition. The living teacher was thought of as an elder brother, guiding and encouraging the neophyte.

Entering such a course of teaching was always accompanied by certain initiatic rites. The teacher was a spiritual father or brother initiating the disciple into a spiritual birth, into an all-important and, for the individual, highly personal experience. Ideally, all teaching of this kind was by word of mouth and adapted to the particular capabilities of the hearer. The written word would only serve as a 'support' to the oral teaching.

From this it will be seen how very different Western concepts of education are. In the West education has completely lost its sacred character. It is 'profane' in the literal meaning of that word, 'outside the sphere of the sacred'; cut off from any links with principial truth. Its ambition is 'practical', its content materialistic and utilitarian, and its audience universal. Every impersonal technique is eagerly employed to reduce the status of a teacher to that of a mere technician and the pupil to that of an empty vessel waiting to be filled with whatever is deemed likely to promote material progress.

Traditional education as it once existed can never be restored, but by studying it the West may still be able to move away from its present disastrously inadequate methods and find new ways of transmitting Temple's 'great and fundamental truths.'

Like all concepts discussed by Guénon, Tradition is elusive and shadowy and it is very difficult to find a definition in his writings. Even in the chapter entitled 'What is Meant by Tradition?' in his *Introduction to the Study of the Hindu Doctrines*, we find a baffling series of generalizations. Guénon was reluctant to provide clear definitions for any of the major concepts with which he was concerned, and this is notably true of Tradition, which in his vocabulary had little to do with any of the meanings of the word in current use: tradition as opposed to Scripture, or 'Traditional', meaning what was assumed to have been practiced for many years past, as in the phrase 'traditional forms of worship'. He inveighed against the use of the word in the plural, as in the traditions of a political party or a school or institution. Tradition was essentially that body of knowledge and self-understanding which is common to all men of all ages and nationalities. Its expression and clarification forms the basis of all traditional wisdom and its application the basis of all traditional societies. It is supra-temporal in origin, the link which unites man as manifestation to his unmanifest origin.

As we have seen, Vedanta in its Advaita formulation—the one adopted by Guénon—is at the extreme end of the spectrum in that it aims at the greatest possible impersonality, the most complete separation between man in the manifest universe and the Principial Unity. The underlying structure of his presentation is strongly influenced by his mathematical training.

As a good Muslim he endeavored to express this Reality in terms which are totally objective, having nothing whatsoever of anthropomorphism in them. The encounter with Ultimate Reality can only be achieved by 'direct intellectual intuition' or pure thought—which is again a concept not unfamiliar to mathemati-cians and would seem to be based on analogical reasoning. The fun-damental science of knowledge is analogous to geometry. So pure intellectual intuition can create analogical links between the one and the many, always maintaining a total separation between ideas derived from the phenomenal world and the Ultimate Reality. This is strikingly demonstrated when Guénon dismisses the notion of 'creation', which has occupied so much of Western thought. For Guénon 'creation' implies purposive action and is thus anthropomorphic in character, whereas manifestation—the making known to the senses of what is and always has been—can be considered as suprapersonal.

However, Guénon is a faithful enough student of Vedanta to admit that the way he presents it is only one viewpoint on Ultimate Reality and is by no means exclusive of others, but merely complementary to them. This refusal to be restricted by any exclusive systematic formulation is insisted on repeatedly by Guénon as an essential feature of all Traditional teaching. Thus Tradition is analogous to the Logos or uncreated word emanating from the *Gottheit* of Eckhart or the *hypertheousios* of Dionysius. This may be implied by the word tradition itself, which simply means that which is handed down. This deposit to be handed down does not stem from any human source, however remote. It is implicit in being human, it is the invisible link between the manifest universe, including man, and the Ultimate Reality, the Principial Truth which sustains it and from which the world derives such 'reality' as it possesses, contingent and relative and subjected to time and space as it is.

We may be helped towards an understanding of this concept by referring to the kabbalistic notion of *Adam Kadmon*, the perfect man, whose union with the Principial Truth was full and complete, and represented distinction without division within the Principial Unity. It is worth recalling also, as Guénon does in *Traditional Forms and Cosmic Cycles*, that the word Adam is usually considered to be derived from the Hebrew word *adamah* or earth, which is not the usual word for earth, which is *erets*. *Adamah* is used for a special red clay, the basic root being *dam*, which means both red and blood. Red earth has a very special place in alchemy as the *prima materia* from which all was fashioned. The connection between the Latin *humus*, earth or soil, and humanity is another clue.

In early Christian theology similar ideas were current in the 'Recapitulation' theories of St Irenaeus. This is the belief that God summed up all that he intended perfect humanity to be in Jesus, the second Adam. The Adam who was recapitulated in Jesus is of course the *Adam Kadmon*, the primordial man; in kabbalistic terms the first configuration of the divine light emanating from the essence of the *En-sof* or Principial Unity. This *Adam Kadmon* is in Masonic teaching the source of all tradition and taught his sons sacred geometry, the most fundamental of all the sacred sciences. So all true traditional knowledge is supra-historical.

The nature of the All and the subsequent separation of man and the Ultimate Reality is paralleled by the Vedantic concept of manifestation, which avoids any personal cause of multiplicity and avoids dualism by implying that the whole manifestation of the cosmos has only a relative and contingent reality, man's essential task being not to redeem it or to restore a lost unity (something which in Vedanta thought has never really been lost), but to be delivered from it.

However, this is not to imply that Guénon or those in the tradition of Vedanta thought are indifferent to what happens in the realm of manifestation. As a means of deliverance we should all strive to live in conformity with the Tradition in all our activities on earth, and to use it as the source of authentic relationship with the Ultimate Reality. There is a Traditional Society and there are Sacred 'Sciences' and nothing that is lacks potential relationship with Ultimate Reality.

In order to elucidate this concept Guénon uses the symbol of weaving. The world of manifestation is like the web, the warp being the vertical descent of unchanging truth and the weft the horizontal expansion, the variable, contingent product of human reason and historical circumstances, the whole representing the seamless robe in which the cosmos and its mysteries are enveloped.

Man, and so also his activities, are to be found as it were in their authenticity at the intersection of the vertical and the horizontal, the place where Principial Unity can be restored. The cross and the crisis are implicit in man and in no other being. As we have already suggested, a sacred anthropology would deny in essence any evolutionary notions. This is not to deny the possibility of biological evolution but simply, once again, to reiterate that always and everywhere, amidst all his ethnic and cultural diversity, man has always had one thing in common: a sense of the Invisible or *istigkect* (the 'Isness'), to use a word coined by Eckhart, from which he stems and to which he is destined to return. This spiritual imprint is what defines man as man. This conviction of relationship or parentage basic to man implies a natural hierarchy and this sense of order is of the essence in all traditional teaching.

Guénon, like Coleridge, believed in being aware of the etymology of the words we use since in so doing we can clarify our thoughts and discover in words something of their intrinsic potency. If we attempt to do this for the word 'order' we are immediately led into a rich field of meaning. The basic root is the Sanskrit *ar/or* which has the meaning of striving upwards, and in this it is obviously connected with the Latin word *ordire,* to begin, and related to the word 'origin'. Consequent upon this is the concept of things happening in a certain 'order', successively and not simultaneously. We are not concerned here with the concept of time and space but with their metaphysical counterparts in a non-dualist sense. This sequentiality is reflected in the world of manifestation as temporal sequence and spatial extension.

Among the traditional sciences, geometry and its practical derivative, architecture, are the basic sciences from which all others descend. Order in architecture is defined as 'a system of parts in established proportions'. Events do not occur in a random or haphazard way but in accordance with a certain necessary sequence, displaying symmetry and balance in which all the parts have their proper position and proportion in order to create a harmonious and balanced whole.

These resonances emanating from the word 'order' are essential for our understanding of what a traditional social order might be. The word society and its related words come from a Sanskrit root *sak*, to follow; so society implies sequence (from the same Sanskrit root), and hence the notion of hierarchy is fundamental to traditional society. Hierarchy in essence means that the rule of the sacred is to be given primacy over all other aspects of reality. For the sacred is identical with that Ultimate Reality, the *Nirguna Brahman* of Vedantist thought.

The analogy between society and the human body is common to both East and West. It is vividly exemplified in the Rig Veda's description of the origin of castes. When Brahma created man he created four men: first Brahman, who emerged from Brahma's mouth, to whom were given the Vedas or Sacred Scriptures. Next Kshatriya emerged from Brahma's right arm. His role was to protect his brother Brahman so that he might expound the Vedas and carry out his priestly duties in safety. Next to emerge was Vaishya, who emerged from Brahma's right thigh. His work was to nourish and provide for the needs of his two brothers. Finally, Shudra emerged from the right foot of Brahma, and he was to be the servant of the other three. The symbolism is strikingly clear.

This division of function is closely paralleled in the West by the medieval notion of the three estates of Clergy, Nobility, and the People, this last corresponding to the last two in the Hindu version. The fact that all four emerged from Brahma implies that they all reflect to a greater or lesser degree his divine nature, thus emphasizing that all work, all occupations which conform with the Primordial Tradition are sacred. Another analogous notion is the notion of the Mystical Body of Christ which exerted such a powerful cohesive force in medieval society. Amongst many expositions perhaps the most relevant is that of St Paul in his first letter to the Corinthians, chapter twelve. Paul first points out that men are endowed by the Spirit with a variety of gifts and makes an analogous reference to the human body, remarking how foolish it would be if one part of the body quarreled with another part or tried to opt out of its membership. But he then goes on to tell his readers that this is no mere analogy, it is a sober serious and actual fact: 'You are the body of Christ.' This community is the pattern for all community at every level, the binding power is the spirit. Here we can see a differentiation of function and an 'order' which, if the whole is to function as it should, must be recognized and adhered to. As has already been pointed out, all grades from the highest to the lowest are mutually responsible and dependent on one another, a hierarchy of equals in which the head is *primas inter pares*.

How far this is from the reality of modern Western society is obvious. In what way does it affect the concept of democracy, a modern shibboleth that is in direct contradiction to all traditional teaching? Where have we gone wrong? Surely by confusing levels. At the metaphysical level we may say 'all men are equal in the sight of God'; but to transfer this statement to the manifest world and its ordering is to fly in the face of the obvious truth that men are in no sense equal at this manifest level. They vary in a great variety of ways and these variations are an inevitable part of the human condition, which partakes, as does all else, in the imperfection and diversity of this state. We have offered men power, without enquiring whether they have sufficient means to employ it with responsibility.

Traditional society will not be achieved by a nostalgic attempt to re-create a vanished past. Guénon was always warning against this kind of misapprehension. There is no way back, there is equally no way out, but there is a way through. Man's infinite worth lies solely in his freedom to become what he is, to realize his potential. Traditional social order helps him in this spiritual task. We cannot turn the clock back or stop the world in order to get off it. But we can see clearly the way in which we are all infected with the current Western ataxia and endeavor to bring our own actions into conformity with the natural social order. This is one of the main functions of an elite, who are not self-appointed or even necessarily aware of the fact that they have been 'chosen' to contribute to a change of direction on the part of the West: 'The world is ruled by letting things take their course. It cannot be ruled by interfering.'[1]

1. *Tao Te Ching*, chap. 48.

4

THE SPIRAL STAIRCASE

COSMIC CYCLES & THE REIGN OF QUANTITY

THE DILEMMA to be confronted in this chapter has been vividly described by C. G. Jung:

> When someone gets his business in a mess, he naturally considers how he can set it on its feet again, and he applies all the remedies that are designed to restore his languishing business to health. But what happens when all these remedies have been tried, when contrary to all reasonable expectations, the situation only slithers from bad to worse? In that case he will be compelled to give up the use of these so-called reasonable methods as speedily as possible. My patient and perhaps our whole age is in this situation. Anxiously he asks me 'What can I do?' And I must answer, 'I don't know either.' I reply that mankind has got into these blind alleys before, countless times during the course of evolution, and no one knew what to do because everybody was busy hatching out clever plans to meet the situation. No one had the courage to admit that they had all taken the wrong turning. And then suddenly things somehow began to move again, so that the same old humanity still exists, though somewhat different from before....
>
> The great events of world history are at bottom profoundly unimportant. In the last analysis the essential thing is the life of the individual. This alone makes history, here alone do the great transformations first take place, and the whole future, the history of the world ultimately spring as a gigantic summation from the

hidden sources in individuals. In our most private and most subjective lives we are not only the passive witnesses of our age, and its sufferers, but also its makers. We make our own epoch.[1]

With this in mind let us address ourselves to the subject of history, a subject which has become of cardinal importance to the West but which for Guénon and Eastern philosophy is of only secondary importance.

For the Greeks history meant the whole unfolding of the manifest world in time and space, embracing both man and nature, and was best symbolized by the circle. For the Jews, whose historical vision was limited to their own nation, history was seen as linear, a temporal succession of events leading to a known end: the promised land and the establishment of an eternal kingdom backed by a covenant with God. For the Christian the horizontal straight line which they inherited from their Jewish predecessors was bisected by a vertical line which in a sense was analogous to the covenant experience of the Jews, but which was not only ongoing, but also finally and decisively terminated the historical process. For Eastern tradition the most expressive symbol is that of the spiral which combines an open-endedness with an element of repetition.

For modern secular man history has been swallowed up in the passage of time, and the best symbol is that of a fast flowing stream: 'Time like an ever rolling stream bears all its sons away.' Today the stream is felt as a raging torrent and we are like canoeists in it, precariously endeavoring, while travelling at top speed to an unknown end, to avoid the innumerable rocks, whirlpools, snags, and eddies that we encounter on the way.

History is for better or worse a Western invention. In his endeavor to hold up this cataract of passing time, to salvage from it some fragments before we and they are swept away for ever, Western man has rediscovered nostalgia. The cult of nostalgia, besides acknowledging that the speed of life was formerly less hectic and certain values, now lost, still existed *illo tempore,* is really modern man's immature effort to return to the womb, to an imagined state of

---

1. C.G. Jung, *Civilization in Transition.* Collected Works, vol. 10, pp148–9.

security and innocence, rather than face the intolerable burdens of the present. But such nostalgia—that pain of being deprived of one's *nostos* or homecoming—is of no avail. Few in the urbanized industrial West have any sense of belonging, or of being rooted and grounded in a particular place. Family solidarity and loyalty to one's ancestors are almost unknown and certainly not considered to be an essential ingredient of a happy life.

The alienation from his human roots is symbolical of man's increasing alienation from his spiritual roots which increases as the cosmic cycle moves further and further away from its spiritual origin and source. Alienation implies separation at every level. Starting with the spiritual level, man is alienated from his spiritual father. This is next reflected in his attempt to create a false family known as the nation, with a purely human 'father of his country' who cannot be any substitute for a relationship with the primal source of all humanity. Efforts to regain the lost Paradise by purely human secular devices built on the concept of the nation-state, by means of a League of Nations or the United Nations, are doomed to fail because the very concept of 'nation' is inadequate and illusory. The only adequate pattern for mankind is the family. This family view has been dramatically illustrated by the Russian philosopher N.F. Fyodorov (1828–1903) for whom the remembrance of our dead ancestors was the task of man and thus a recognition of his status as a son:

> The only true religion is the cult of ancestors, i.e., the universal cult of all fathers considered as one father, unseparated from the Triune God yet unconfused with Him in whom the separation of sons and daughters, as well as their differentiations, is deified.... The separation of our forefathers from the Triune God is the same perversion as the limitation of a religion's universality.[2]

This is a far cry from the alienated nostalgia of lost and rootless people. But it is very close to the traditional conception of an organic

---

2. N.F. Fyodorov, *Filosofia obshchevo de la* [Philosophy of the Common Task], quoted in *Ultimate Questions,* ed. by A. Schmemann (NY, 1965; London, 1977), pp176–7.

community rooted in an ever-present past which symbolizes its links with the eternal reality.

The Greek view of the circular nature of history embodied in the myth of the eternal return is in direct opposition to the Judeo-Christian linear view of history, and also, of course, to the Eastern view of cosmic cycles. St Augustine dismissed the Greek view when, in his *De Civitate Dei*, he wrote:

> The wicked walk in a circle, not because their life (as they think) runs circularly, but because their false doctrine runs round in a circular maze' (BK XI, chap. 13).

But Augustine was an early proponent of what was soon to become the predominant Western view of history. Perhaps it was inevitable that the Jewish linear view should be adopted by the Christian Church, for in one sense the coming of the Christ or Messiah was the great event at the end of the line stretching from Abraham through Moses and the delivery from Egypt and the entrance into the promised land. But for the Jews and for many Christians it was no more than one event in a continuous series. The struggle to transcend this linear concept of the *Pilgrim's Progress*, or man's journey from cradle to the grave, has never been fully won by the Church. The transcendent element in our daily lives has too easily been relegated to before birth or after death. The full implication of the vertical descent of the transcendent into the realm of manifestation has never been fully realized and was largely limited to the experience of individuals.

In this, as in so many other things, the West can find a compensatory emphasis in the priority given by the East to the transcendent, which is the hallmark of all traditional thought. As Thomas Merton said in his introduction to a translation of the *Bhagavad Gītā*:

> The Gita brings to the West a salutary reminder that our highly activistic and one-sided culture is faced with a crisis that may end in self-destruction because it lacks the inner depth of an authentic metaphysical consciousness.... If in the West God can no longer be experienced as other than 'dead', it is because of an inner split and self-alienation which have characterized the

Western mind in its single-minded dedication to only half of life: that which is exterior, objective and quantitative.[3]

Guénon's last major work was called *The Reign of Quantity and the Signs of the Times*. In it he describes with great insight the progressive separation of Western civilization from its traditional rootedness in the Ultimate Reality. The concept of time has suffered from the same compulsive quantification; witness the staggering calculations now current on the age of the universe and the size of the cosmos, calculations which are in essence meaningless and serve only to make man feel trivial, ephemeral, worthless, and so entitled to act with complete irresponsibility. Pascal, contemplating the infinite space of the heavens, was terrified by their eternal silence, but it was a holy and life-enhancing awe. For him, but not for modern man, the Heavens declared the glory of God.

If we compare modern society with that of any Eastern nation or of past civilizations elsewhere, we shall see an entirely different way of dealing with the passage of time. Of such societies Mircea Eliade has written:

> What impresses us above all in these archaic systems is the abolition of concrete time and furthermore their anti-historic character. The refusal to preserve the memory of the past, even the immediate past, would seem to indicate a particular anthropology. It is in short the refusal of archaic man to see himself as an historic being and his refusal to attribute any value to memory and so to any abnormal events (i.e., those which have no archetypal counterpart). In the end we descry in all the ceremonies and rites and their attendant points of view *the wish to devalue time*. Pushed to their furthest limits all these rites and attitudes which we have described can be summed up in the following statement: If one pays no attention to it, time does not exist.[4]

Such a view is certainly typical of the Vedanta and acceptable as part of the Primordial Tradition, and is not at all inconsistent with the

---

3. Thomas Merton, *Asian Journal* (NY, 1975) p349.
4. Eliade, *Myth of the Eternal Return*, p104.

Western tradition in its pure form. For if, instead of incor-porating the vertical descent of the Christ into the linear procession as one event among many others, similar in kind to those of Jewish history, it is seen as an event outside time, creating within it an ever-present Now in which history is superseded and direct trans-cendence of the time process is achieved by the entering into the eternal present—the timeless moment in which alone we can truly be, for Now is the time of salvation—then indeed time will truly be seen to be an illusion.

Such an understanding and experience would be the conscious recovery of the state of primal innocence described by Eliade. The complete realization of both these states lies outside the realm of time and the manifest universe—the first representing the Paradisal state before the Fall, and the latter, final deliverance and absorption in the Beatific Vision. It is the awareness of this possibility, both in our past and in our future, that motivates man to seek here and now this transcendence of all the contingencies and limitations of his state as part of the phenomenal world. Indeed, we can only truly live as authentic human beings in that eternal present recreated moment by moment by our recognition of the temporal and spatial illusion.

For Guénon, as for all traditional wisdom, truth has to be lived by the whole man, which explains his frequent dismissals of the inadequacy of rational thought, of thinking about things. As the Russian philosopher Nicolas Berdyaev says:

> In reality cognition is emotional and passionate in character. It is a spiritual struggle for meaning... the significance of a philosophy is decided by the passionate intensity of the philosopher as a man, as one who is present behind the effort to know. It is decided by the intensity of the will to truth and meaning, it is the whole man who takes knowledge of a thing.[5]

No man could have shown more passionate intensity in the search for truth than Guénon—a passion all the more remarkable by its total lack of any desire to be seen as the personal originator of that

---

5. N. Berdyaev, *The Beginning and the End* (1952), p37.

truth. As his Arab name implies, he was a true image of John the Forerunner, the Announcer.

So, once again, we are compelled to see that any rational enquiry into the meaning of history *in toto* is pointless, since as Jung points out, history is ultimately made by individuals, not vice versa. But the whole process of manifestation has nevertheless a momentum and a logic of its own, symbolized as we shall see by the doctrine of Cosmic Cycles, the Spiral Staircase. Within this ineluctable process each individual, living in his own time and out of it at the same time, has to discover his or her own meaning.

It is quite striking how Guénon and Berdyaev complement one another. Guénon is detached, objective, and wholeheartedly concerned with the Principial Truth, which alone can give reality and meaning to the phenomenal world; Berdyaev, emotional as only a Slav can be, is subjective and passionately concerned with individual man's search for meaning in concrete terms, personal and inescapably related to his situation as the centerpiece of the Great Triad. In the symbolism of ancient Rome, they represent the two faces of Janus, the oldest of the gods and the holiest and most exalted, who faced both ways, towards and away from man, and so eminently represented man's special status *vis-à-vis* the eternal world. This twofold stance reminds us that, as Berdyaev said,

> Knowledge of the divine life is not attainable by means of abstract philosophical thought ... but only by means of a concrete myth which conceives the divine life as a passionate destiny of concrete and active persons, the divine Hypostases.[6]

This at first sight seems very far from Guénon's impersonal insistence on shedding all personal emotional elements, of which one must be stripped if one is to achieve that 'pure intellectual intuition' which he sees as the sole way of attainment. But this very stripping and detachment is itself an entirely personal undertaking and one which demands a total personal commitment. If by Berdyaev's 'concrete myth' we understand, as I think we are entitled to, Guénon's understanding of the function of all dogmatic formulations and

---

6. N. Berdyaev, ibid., pp 51–2.

religious doctrines, we can understand the necessity of anthropomorphic language and the symbolic representation of Principial Truth by means of rites and ceremonies, which are, as it were, its local dress and language. Moreover, the entire contents of the phenomenal world are a reflection of part of the contents of the all in all, the Pleroma. Their manifestation can by symbolically described as the drama enacted between God and Himself, the Son of Man is also the Son of God.

But as Berdyaev says, all 'this is in the sphere of mythology,' an attempt to express the inexpressible, for no words are adequate here. However, provided we remain aware that words can be no more than an approximation, at least we do the best we can, and, provided we constantly recall their true nature as clothes, not the body clothed, then in them we possess a valid and authentic key to the mystery of the metaphysics of history.

Guénon and Berdyaev, who came from widely different backgrounds, were both, to borrow a phrase from Nietzsche, 'aristocratic radicals', aristocratic not by birth or lineage but through being men of rare intellectual and spiritual quality who naturally felt themselves to be members of a human élite. We are aristocrats in the inner man, as Eckhart says, by virtue of that true self, the *Funkelein* or *Scintilla*, the Divine Spark, that which 'I' hear and heed, as in Psalm 85: *Audiam qui loquiter in me, dominus Deus (*I hear who speaks within me, the Lord God).[7]

Both Guénon and Berdyaev possessed an all-embracing concern for the fate of humanity and a humble perseverance in sharing their insights. Both left far behind the cultural and religious environments in which they were raised and fearlessly followed the search for truth wherever it led them. Both were frequently misunderstood by those whom they had left behind, but nevertheless never became resentful or arrogant. They were in Paris at the same time but I have found no evidence that they ever met, though they must have been aware of one another's writings. Guénon, who was not noticeably lenient towards Christian thought in its degenerate state, nevertheless believed that the Eastern Church had retained somewhat more

---

7. *Meister Eckhart, A Modern Translation*, R.B. Blakney (NY, 1957), pp 74 ff.

of the authentic tradition than the West. A comparative study of their work would surely prove fruitful.

Both believed that it was possible for man here and now to encounter God or Principial Truth, and Guénon would surely have agreed with Berdyaev when he wrote,

> What is needed is not so much to set certain ends before one and to realize them in the practical world making use of evil means in doing so, as to display, express and radiate a creative energy of one's own, in knowledge, in love, in a sense of community, in freedom and in beauty, and to be self-determined in the strength of one's awareness of the end.[8]

All this is, for this student at least, implicit in the whole of Guénon's writings, the study of which remains sterile and mere intellectual trifling unless it motivates us to search for the Ultimate Reality and live it as we search for it. This will involve above all the recognition that while, as Guénon always maintained, it is absolutely necessary to be an active participant in one of the great traditional religions, nevertheless all systems, dogmas, doctrinal and credal formulations are of secondary importance in that they are only different ways of viewing the Ultimate Truth. By their very nature they can only be landmarks or boundary fences defining one's position, rather than infallible and total enunciations of the truth.

The search for deliverance alone can give meaning to the history of the individual, and so, collectively to the history of a nation or a civilization. Deliverance, not from the fatigues and constraints of our earthly life, but from illusion and falsehood; the attainment of what in Hindu terminology is called *moksha* and in the Christian tradition 'The Beatific Vision', defined by Karl Rahner as

> the full and definitive experience of the direct self-communication of God himself to the individual human being when by free grace, God's will has become absolute and attained its full realization.[9]

---

8. Berdyaev, *Meaning and History* (1936), p 253.
9. *Sacramentum Mundi Encyclopedia of Theology* (1975), 'Beatific Vision'.

History, like religion and theology, is for Guénon secondary to the encounter with Reality. Ideally they should all be the means whereby this encounter is facilitated. They are also, as it were, necessary extensions and applications of that encounter in the realm of manifestation, through which the realization of the Divine Will or *Prajāpati* in the form of *Manu* appropriate to each cycle can occur (cf. *Man and His Becoming*, chap. 4).

Guénon has often been accused of being indifferent to history, and indeed in the Greek sense of the word he is indifferent to its quantitative elements. But he was interested in history in the sense implied by the German word *Geschichte,* which implies that 'the event' as the result of an irresistible working of forces in its impact leads to one inescapable conclusion: a choice was made. History is only valid as presenting man with a series of crises that demand his decision. These decisions can only be made correctly if he is anchored in Transcendent Reality and able to recognize that:

> The greatest virtue is to follow Tao and Tao alone.
> The Tao is elusive and intangible.
> Oh, it is intangible and elusive, and yet within is image.
> Oh, it is elusive and intangible and yet within is form.
> Oh, it is dim and dark, and yet within is essence.
> This essence is very real and therein lies faith.
> From the beginning until now the name has never been forgotten.
> Thus I perceive the creation.[10]

In the sacred sciences, history as the West understands it, with all its implications of temporal progression and endless evolution, has no place. The traditional understanding of the passage and content of time in the manifest world is based on the concept of the Cosmic Cycle which has almost entirely disappeared from Western thought. It is so much in opposition to Western adherence to the linear image that it is often dismissed as archaic, static, unchristian, or by some other derogatory epithet. It may be that the word cycle is misleading since it may be taken to mean endless repetition within a close circle. A far better pictorial representation is the spiral, in

---

10. *Tao Te Ching,* chap. 21.

which each revolution after a long apparent descent finishes higher than the previous cycle.

In traditional Vedanta teaching the most comprehensive cycle is the *Kalpa*, which denotes the total development of a manifestation such as that of our present world. The *Kalpa* is divided into fourteen *Manvantaras*. In the current *Kalpa* we are nearing the end of the Seventh *Manvantara*. In this system the duration of each *Manvantara is* 64,800 years. According to another system of calculation, the *Kalpa* is divided into a thousand *Mahayugas* or 'great ages' lasting 12,000 years each. Each *Mahayuga* is divided into four yugas. This division into four yugas is constant in both systems, since *Manvantaras* are also so divided. These four ages correspond to the Western tradition of the four ages of gold, silver, bronze, and iron, as described by Hesiod in his *Works and Days,* and later by Virgil and Ovid.

Each age, both as regards its duration and its *dharma* (i.e., the degree to which obedience to the primal law of Manu obtains), is divided in the proportion of 4:3:2:1, i.e., the Golden Age lasts four times as long as the Iron Age and in it the primal law is four times as fully obeyed as it is in the Iron Age. According to Mircea Eliade each yuga or age is preceded and followed by twilight periods of 400, 300, 200, and 100 years respectively. Thus in this form of calculation, the *Krita-Yuga* or Golden Age lasts 4,800 years, the *Treta-Yuga* or Silver Age lasts 3,600 years, the *Dvapara-Yuga* or Bronze Age lasts 2,400 years, and the *Kali-Yuga* 1,200 years, so that the entire *Mahayuga* or complete cycle lasts 12,000 years. The last stage of the *Kali-Yuga* and the completion *of* the whole cycle is attained in a period of dissolution: *Pralaya*, when manifestation is dissolved and reabsorbed to start a fresh cycle. *Pralaya* in Kashmiri Saivism is also the transcendental phase of consciousness, the passive phase, the potential period when all manifestation is dormant, which is entirely appropriate to the end of one cycle and the beginning of another.[11]

In the formulation in terms of *Manvantara* which is that favored by Guénon, each *Manvantara* lasts 64,800 years (i.e., five 'great years'

---

11. Important elucidation can be found in: T. Bernard, *Philosophical Foundations of India* (1945) and in the works of Georgel (see bibliography).

of 12,960 ordinary years each, which is close to the generally calculated length of the Precession of the Equinox). Another division of the *Manvantara* is into thirty Cosmic Cycles of 2,160 years. These in turn can be considered as made up of shorter cycles, until we come down to the cycle of an individual life-span and the seven ages of man. Equally, the cosmic or supra-terrestrial realm undergoes the same cyclical evolution as exemplified by the motion of the celestial bodies.

What are we in the West today to make of all these, and many, many other elaborate calculations? The essential fact is not the predictive possibilities opened up by such calculations. What is important is the way in which they provide us with a general symbolic framework for the understanding of our destiny in the world and of the world position at a given time. In all such concepts of history one finds at the beginning a Golden Age outside time, and at the end, after the irruption of the forces of evil from the lower world, a final consummation symbolized by the descent of the heavenly city and the establishment of the Divine Kingdom that will inaugurate a new *Kalpa*. So, as Guénon points out, metaphysically, beginnings and endings are both illusory. Any preoccupation with precise dates and historical data risks missing completely the scope of Eastern vision as shown us by Guénon, by limiting all our interest and concern to the historical process within the manifest world with all its limitations and contingencies.

The Western mind today with its ingrained adherence to the linear concept of progress, once described as an elastic highway forever stretching out before man who can never reach its end, is constitutionally reluctant to consider any other way of looking at things. As J. F. C. Harrison says, we are unwilling to consider such a notion seriously because

> it is couched largely in the language of theology and employs technical terms with which we are no longer familiar. Our vocabulary is provided by the sociologist and the psychologist rather than the theologian. We have to make a conscious effort even to grasp what the millenarians are saying.... In our present secular age many people find it difficult to take seriously a belief in the

millennium and by projecting this disbelief into their view of the past, they preclude themselves from a sympathetic understanding ... we simply fail to see the force or logic of something which does not rest on our own intellectual assumptions, and so we are incredulous.[12]

Mutatis mutandis, this seems to be the difficulty confronting most people when they first encounter Guénon's work. Once again Berdyaev challenges us as he writes:

> Man's celestial history and destiny predetermine his terrestrial. The theme of universal history is given us in the heavenly prologue. But what do we mean by celestial history? It is the true metaphysical foundation of history. Heaven and the heavenly life in which the historical process originates constitute the deepest interior spiritual life. For heaven is not a remote transcendental and unobtainable sphere; it is part of the utmost depths of our spiritual fife. When we dive below the surface and penetrate into these depths we then really commune with celestial life. In them is stored a spiritual experience which differs from that of terrestrial reality and which represents a deeper and more spacious stratum of being. In it, in this interior spiritual reality ... lies the source of history.[13]

It hardly needs to be said that the depths to which Berdyaev refers are not identical with the depths of the psyche of modern 'depth' psychology but refer rather to the *dahara,* that little empty space at the center of the spiritual heart symbolized by the lotus or *padma,* a space created by *akāsha,* the principle of emptiness sometimes translated as 'ether'. Here in the empty center is the dwelling place of Atma-Brahman. Obviously, we are attempting to express the inexpressible and all spatial and temporal metaphors are inapplicable, but the reality remains.

Guénon insists on the transcendent nature of Absolute Reality, the Brahma without a name, and Berdyaev would agree entirely, for

---

12. J.F.C. Harrison, *The Second Coming* (n.d.), p3.
13. Berdyaev, *The Meaning of History* (1936), p44.

as he said, 'Metaphysics can only be the apprehension of spirit in spirit and through spirit.' Ultimate Reality, while remaining one and self-contained, is yet the source of that limited Reality which we possess, that in it which is alone indestructible. But as Berdyaev also points out, 'As a system of concepts, metaphysics is an impossibility, it is possible only as the symbolism of spiritual experience.'

The peculiar contribution of the West today, as Guénon frequently suggested, will not be in achieving the originality it so highly prizes, but in rediscovering, relearning and reapplying what once it knew and has forgotten but which the East has never forgotten. All that is patent in Eastern thought and only latent in the West has to be re-thought in terms of the specifically Western viewpoint, which is that of Catholic Christianity. If we believe that each of the great authentic vehicles of the Primordial Tradition has a specific viewpoint and so a special contribution to offer to the understanding of the whole, then we might say with Schelling that 'Christianity introduced the notion of history into the relationship of man and God.' After the coming of the Christ, the metaphysical link between the eternal and the temporal, between the Primordial Unity and manifestation in the phenomenal world, was made evident and Man was confirmed as the incarnation or embodiment of that union.

'History,' says Berdyaev, 'is a progression. It possesses an inner significance and mystery, a point of departure and a goal, a center and a purpose.' That center and that purpose are most clearly revealed by the doctrine of Cosmic Cycles, which are the most comprehensive and meaningful symbol of the inner reality of the historical process referred to by Berdyaev. His three periods are a wonderful epitome of what Guénon describes at length in *The Reign of Quantity* in such striking detail.

> First a period that is one of direct integral and organic experience in some settled historical order ... here thought is static ... secondly there is a period of fateful and menacing schism and disruption when the foundations of an established order are tottering. It is in this collapse of organic structure and vital rhythm that the historical process originates.... The result of

this schism and disruption is that the knowing subject no longer feels himself directly and wholly a part of the historical object; and this gives birth to the speculations of historical science.... Thirdly there is a period that implies a return to the 'historical'. Thus when I say that catastrophic moments are particularly propitious for the elaboration of a philosophy of history, I have in view those catastrophes when the human spirit, having experienced the collapse of a given historical order and the moment of schism and disintegration, is able to appose and op-pose these two moments . . . in order to arrive at a third spiritual state which induces a particularly acute consciousness, a parti-cular aptitude for speculation and a corresponding aspiration towards the mysteries of the 'historical'.[14]

One can imagine that the collapse of European civilization in the Second World War may well have been such a moment for Guénon, inducing him to write his masterpiece *The Reign of Quantity*, which concludes:

So it is that if one wishes to penetrate to the deepest level of reality, one can say in all objective truth that 'the end of the world' is never and can never be anything but the end of an illusion.

---

14. Berdyaev, ibid., pp3–5.

5

THE PRIMAL VISION

SYMBOLS AND TRUTH

As in everything else, Guénon's approach to the subject of symbols starts from purely metaphysical concepts and descends gradually into the realm of manifestation. His exposition is often couched in a negative form, as in his chapter on 'Symbolism and Anthropo-morphism' in *Introduction to the Study of the Hindu Doctrines,* in which he points out the failure of many Westerners to see beyond the symbol itself to the truth it represents, a failure that gives rise to idolatry and anthropomorphism. This attitude has for a long time bedeviled Western understanding of Hinduism, which has been accused of worshipping idols.

Taking for granted the impossibility of any starting point being other than arbitrary, we may begin with the notion common to all traditional thought: that of pure impalpable Ether, unmanifest essence, in the Vedanta *Atman* and in the Kabbalah *Avir.* This impalpable Ether is made manifest by its concentration into a point in the geometrical sense of the word, as having location but no magnitude. This point, which is equivalent to the number one, is the starting point of all manifestation or extension, as the number one is the starting point of all numbers. Both may be said to be as purely qualitative as anything within the realm of manifestation can be, since all that is emerges from them; they are the grain of mustard seed.

The symbolism of space around a point is the first modification of the primal chaos, which can only be geometrically determined. A directional grid is, as it were, imposed upon it, and it is cruciform, for the cross is perhaps the most fundamental of all symbols. It is the universal symbol for the ordering of space, the vertical and horizontal arms being infinitely extended. But in order to encompass three-dimensional reality as we experience it, another cross representing the third dimension has to be added and the whole enclosed in a circle whose diameter is infinite. Thus is chaos ordered.

This notion is also to be found in the Western tradition. Clement of Alexandria, for example, wrote in his *Stromateis* that

> from God, the heart of the universe, originate all the infinite extensions, above and below, to the right and to the left, forwards and backwards. Directing his eye to these six extensions in their infinitude as if towards an eternally immutable number, he creates the universe. He is Alpha and Omega, in him are completed the six infinite extensions of time and from him they extend towards the infinite, and herein lies the secret of the number seven.[1]

A quotation from St Augustine's *De Civitate Dei is* another example of the congruence of the Western tradition with its Eastern forms:

> And these [the works of creation] were performed in six days because of the perfection of the number six, one being six times repeated: not that God was tied unto time, and could not have created all at once, and afterwards have bound the motions to time's congruence, but because that number signified the perfection of the work; for six is the first number that is filled by conjunction of the parts, the sixth, the third, and the half: which is one, two, and three; all which conjoined are six.[2]

Modern science and traditional wisdom are uniting in seeing the basic constitution of the universe as being best comprehended as geometric structures of form and proportion, ideas first propounded by Pythagoras, and which certainly were the source, at least in part, of the Christian ideas quoted above. This notion of cosmic harmony and balance is basic to all traditional learning. Plato, when asked what God did in his spare time, said that He

---

1. Quoted in Paul Vuillaud, *La Kabbale juive* (Paris, 1976), vol. 1, pp 215–16.
2. St Augustine, *De Civitate Dei,* BK 10, chap. 30.

geometrizes, and in Masonic teaching Adam is said to have taught his sons geometry.

Arising from the cruciform symbolism there is another and very closely related symbol, that of the center, which was the subject of Guénon's book *The King of the World*. The point where the vertical and horizontal lines intersect is, as Clement suggests, the heart or center where God exists, the location of the ineffable Brahma, the *omphalos* of the Universal Man, *Adam Kadmon*, the central point from which all manifestation unfolds, the point of union with the Principial Unity. In Muslim esotericism it is the Divine Station, that which combines and contrasts antinomies; in Hinduism it is the center of the Lotus. In Far-Eastern tradition it is called the Invariable Middle, the hub of the Cosmic Wheel, the point where *wu-wu-wei*, active inactivity, is exercised, where the Activity of Heaven is directly manifest. It is the place where 'Tao abides in non-action yet nothing is left undone.'

Man in his cruciform appearance is his own symbol and the source of many other symbols relating to the different parts of his body, all of which have a symbolic significance. He is also the model for his sacred structures, for is he not the Temple of the Holy Spirit? But his most important symbolic attribute is his power of speech. In the Judeo-Christian tradition this is the most fertile source of the profoundest symbolism and is no doubt connected with the harmonic or musical nature of the underlying structure of reality. God speaks and we may surely infer that the natural sounds of wind, rain, thunder, the rushing of water, the crackling of fire burning, were all immediately incorporated into the symbolic understanding of reality. Such natural and often incomprehensible sounds, together with the cries of birds and animals, gave man's own voice and power of speech a particular significance.

The Principial Unity is ineffable and beyond language, but human language is the most potent symbol of the creative activity of God. But it is the spoken word, the emanation of spirit, not the rational discourse of modern Western man, that is referred to. The Jewish Tradition speaks of

> a language which expresses the pure thought of God and the letters of his spiritual language are the elements both of the most

fundamental spiritual reality and of the profoundest understanding and knowledge. Abulafia's mysticism is a course in this divine language ... the systematic practice of meditation as taught by him produces a sensation closely akin to that of listening to musical harmonies. The science of combination is a music of pure thought in which the alphabet takes the place of the musical scale.[3]

Such is the kabbalistic formulation of the importance and nature of language. Small wonder therefore that all traditional teaching is oral.

Language is by its very nature symbolic since meaning is mediated by sound; furthermore, it is a gift unique to man alone whereby he is distinguished from all the rest of manifest creation. Language in its rational aspect is an essential part of man in the world of manifestation. Adam was told by God to give every living creature a name, thereby revealing the distinctions to be found in the world of manifestation; but distinction does not imply separation, rather a recognition of authentic differences within the primal unity. Coleridge makes a useful distinction between divisive activities, which he calls keen, and distinctive actions, which he calls subtle:

> Few men of genius are keen; but almost every man of genius is subtle. If you ask the difference between keenness and subtlety, I answer that it is the difference between a point and an edge. To split a hair is no proof of subtlety; for subtlety acts in distinguishing differences—in showing that two things apparently one, are in fact two; whereas to split a hair is to cause division and not to ascertain a difference.[4]

Coleridge, like Guénon and all Eastern thinkers, realized the importance of distinguishing rather than dividing; one of the difficulties of Eastern thought for Westerners is the immensely subtle distinctions that are made by it while always keeping in sight essential

---

3. G. Scholem, *Major Trends in Jewish Mysticism* (1955), p 133.
4. Quoted in Owen Barfield, *What Coleridge Thought* (Wesleyan Univ. Press, Middletown, CT, 1971).

unity. Western thought has followed for many centuries the path of division, that is of quantification, to the almost total exclusion of the concept of unity with distinctions within it. Symbolism is a prime means of retaining unity while discovering a multitude of distinctions. The subtle use of language as a vehicle for symbolic understanding has always been the function of the poet, for whom words are sacred and laden with transcendental worth. In general, however, in the West words have ceased to be sacred and qualitatively loaded; they are used in enormous quantities but always imprecisely and without any sensitivity.

Speech is the authentic activity of man as man confronting his fellow men, and all the phenomenal universe is symbolized by the cross, at the center of which in its cosmic extension he stands—Janus, the Roman god of going out and coming in, always facing two ways, for ever at a crisis point and yet destined to become the sage, the motionless mover of all, at the very point where he stands.

The gift of language is the link that binds men together; but man is also united in his common task, which in traditional societies is considered to be the maintenance, protection and amplification of all that is—conservation in its fullest sense. *Homo faber,* artifex and opifex, derived from two Sanskrit roots, *ar* (to join), and *ap* (work). From these roots has sprung a very wide range of words, including both the English word art and the German 'art' meaning something very different, i.e., descent, innate property, nature. In traditional societies man sees himself not as an originator but rather as one who discovers what was previously present but hidden, reminding us that 'invent' is derived from the Latin word meaning to find or come upon something.

Homo ludens, man in his rhythmic life, works and rests; celebration, feasting, ceremonial relaxation and recreation are all essentially symbolic of the diastole and systole of all life, imaged by God's rest from his creative activity on the seventh day. In classical Chinese philosophy time is essentially a qualitative not a quanti-tative concept having much in common with the Greek *Kairos.* In it the two essential actions of breathing and hence of living have their space, as do the essential activities of man's work and play, which are equally vehicles of art and craft. How far from such a point of view has modern man strayed in his desperate efforts to 'kill time' and the sheer quantity without quality of his leisure activities, which are predominantly passive in nature.

All arts express this pleasurable activity since they are so constituted as to rejoice the souls of men, to raise, by means of their beauty, their spirits beyond the beauties of nature to the Divine Source of all beauty. Art in traditional societies is unknown as a separate activity or feature of any creative act. Everything that was made reflected an eternal and unchangeable reality mediated to man in the multitudinous forms of nature. This attitude was part of his very being, which was outraged by anything that did not exemplify, and in so doing both symbolize and strengthen, the cosmic harmony and balance. The clear-cut distinction between work and play was hardly recognized; there was certainly no preference for one over the other, any more than breathing in can be preferred to breathing out.

One aspect of this celebratory, playful aspect of men's daily life was its symbolic power to sustain the necessary cosmic balance. Dancing, for instance, and all other bodily movements, are both physically pleasurable and also full of potency. Every activity, whether it was directly related to what was necessary for the preservation of life in its physical aspect (which we call work) or whether it was engaged in for pleasure, had also a function of recreation and symbolized the ever-present creator and preserver of all mankind, who, if his eye blinked for one millionth of a second, would plunge the whole cosmos into annihilation.

Homo sapiens. It has been remarked before that man's knowing is in the present continuous tense. In traditional societies all knowledge was sacred. The sacred sciences as developed in the Far East are, in their scope, methods, and intentions, very different from the profane sciences of the West. Once again it is the difference between distinction and division that characterizes them. It may be that Western science has reached a turning point when analysis will finally give way to a new synthesis.

Eastern science has never entered on the path of division and so has not achieved the doubtful advantage of the 'mastery' of nature, but it is now being recognized more and more in the West as a valid and valuable alternative approach. A knowledge aimed at maintaining unity by a series of checks and balances, by the recognition of all things in their 'correspondence'. Guénon frequently emphasizes this word, so it is perhaps worth considering its etymology: *co-respondere*—together, mutually, to make a solemn pact, the last part being related to the Greek word *spondo*, to pour a libation. So in the genuine use of language, when there is correspondence between things, what is meant is something far more than a mere resemblance; rather a fundamental underlying unity that partakes of the sacred. This explanation may provide the reader with a fresh insight into the symbolic nature of words when they are really understood. So, in traditional societies, all the experiences and activities of life were in some way or another connected and symbols of the eternal indivisible reality from which they originated.

Bishop John Taylor, who spent many years in Africa, describes movingly the sense of unity and mutual interdependence that characterizes traditional societies. Writing of the experience of going out on a fishing trip with a group of Ugandan Africans, he concludes his account thus:

> I have recounted this experience at some length because . . . it may help to make significant to the imagination something of that sense of cosmic oneness which is an essential feature of primal religion. Not only is there less separation between subject and object, between self and not self, but fundamentally all things share the same nature and the same interaction one upon another—rocks and forest trees, beasts and serpents, the power of wind and waves upon a ship, the power of a drum over a dancer's body, the power in the mysterious caves of Kokola, the living, the dead and the first ancestors, from the stone to the divinities, a hierarchy of power, but not of being, all are one, all are here, all are now.[5]

I think it is not unfair to say that Guénon underplayed the role of imagination in the formulation of symbols and overstressed their genesis as the means whereby through 'pure intellectual intuition'

5. J.V. Taylor *The Primal Vision* (1963), p 64.

we may apprehend ultimate reality. But this pure intellectual intuition employs, as a stepping stone to its goal, the faculty of imagining, even though in the final achievement of the Beatific Vision all props fall away, all distinctions disappear, and all symbols are swallowed up in the Supreme Identity, the *waḥdat al-wujūd* of Islamic esotericism.

But in the world of manifestation and apparent diversity, symbols discovered by the imagination are the means whereby we make progress in our search, first for relatedness, and then complete apprehension of the Truth and deliverance from the phenomenal world. For as Coleridge says, the supreme function of the imagination is to be

> that reconciling and mediatory power which, incorporating the reason in images of the sense, and organizing (as it were) the flux of the senses by the permanence and self-circling energies of the reason, gives birth to a system of symbols, harmonious in themselves and consubstantial with the truths of which they are the conductors.[6]

A word of warning for Western man may not be out of place here. It is a total misunderstanding of Eastern tradition to affirm, as many have done, that it is world-denying and that the highest good it offers man is speedy deliverance from his earthly existence. Even a superficial reading of the *Tao Te Ching* reveals how concerned it is with the ordering of the here and now world in which we live. It would be nearer the truth to say that Eastern thought has never separated the manifest world from its eternal, unitary counterpart which it reflects in multiple diversity. Reunion with this unitary reality is to be achieved *through* this world, and not by deliverance from it. (Students of the *I Ching* may recall Hexagram 40.) All traditions have had to come to terms with this seeming duality. Advaita Vedanta insists on non-duality, which is not monism, or pantheism, nor is it a complete separation. To hold on to this principle of distinction without division we need the mediation of symbols that provide the essential link between contingence and permanence.

6. Barfield, loc. cit., p112.

The Cosmic Cycle of change reminds us that in this *Kalpa* we are in the final age of dissolution. The primal vision of unity has been shattered beyond restoration, for it was largely unconscious; and if it had not been shattered, the penetration of the material world by rational enquiry would never have taken place, and man would never have been consciously and rationally aware of his situation. The categories of free will and determinism are irrelevant in the cosmic sphere, since the unfolding of the *Kalpa is* inevitable; but always and at any time anyone can consciously decide to seek the Principial Truth, that Truth which is also Way (*Tao*) and Life, and which alone can set us free.

In the totality of manifestation each culture, each tradition and every person has a particular role to play. The various stages of the evolution of consciousness in the West have been chronicled by Erich Neumann in his seminal work *The Origins and History of Consciousness*. While recognizing the symbolic nature of Jungian archetypes and the purely analogical nature of Neumann's description of consciousness, we can discern that there is nevertheless a correspondence between the microcosm of the human psyche and its unfolding, and the evolution of the macrocosm. Moreover, we must agree with Neumann when he writes: 'The evolution of consciousness as a form of creative evolution is the peculiar achievement of Western man.' How could it be otherwise, since psychology has trodden a path parallel to that of all the other branches of profane science in employing analysis, division, systematization and classification as its basis?

We have no choice but to accept the present state of affairs, for good or ill. In so doing we are free to consider how other cultures have developed other and entirely different patterns of behavior and have provided different explanations of them. We shall thus be contributing to the restoration of that cosmic harmony which has been so severely disturbed in the West during the last five hundred years; a disturbance which has been meanwhile rejected by the East. We in the West should welcome the Eastern alternatives and not, like Freud, imagine that there is only one psychological approach applicable to all mankind. Freud's hope of finding traces of the Oedipus complex among the Trobriand Islanders was doomed to be proved false, as were the premises on which *Totem and Taboo* was based. This did not prevent the work from being published without any modification or admission of error—an example of Western obstinacy in maintaining that our culture must become the norm for the whole world. What is true of this one science is true of them all.

We are still immersed in our own culture and only just beginning to realize, as Guénon pointed out on numerous occasions, that our Western profane sciences are all too often a hindrance to true understanding and that they can never be reconciled with the Sacred Sciences.

The Sacred Sciences differ from the profane sciences in that their objective is fundamentally different. As we have said, they are never practiced merely for the sake of acquiring knowledge, which in the case of profane sciences means the accumulation of facts by means of analysis and discrimination. The Sacred Sciences all aim at the demonstration and/or preservation of cosmic balance. In many cases they have a symbolic value. This is especially true of Alchemy. So far from being merely or predominantly an unsuccessful predecessor of modern chemistry, Alchemy is a Sacred Science based on the theory of correspondences and remains constantly aware of the Principial Unity from which the different elements are derived and in the world of manifestation locked in their differentiation.

The central objective of the Alchemist is summed up in the exhortative saying *solve et coagula*. First 'chaotic', 'primal' matter has to be dissolved, i.e. separated, into its constituent elements, and then reassembled (coagulated) into a new arrangement; a process to be repeated until the pattern of perfection is achieved. This process is also understood by Alchemists to be analogous to death and resurrection for the individual, and indicative of the soul's progress through many different states before attaining perfection.

One reader of this book, while it was in the course of composition, described it as 'very cerebral' and others may be inclined to agree. But I hope I have followed, however imperfectly, in Guénon's footsteps. His writing is seldom either prescriptive or predictive; he did not tell people what to do, nor was he in the business of foretelling the future. For him it was as it was for the Far-Eastern sage, who was bidden to give up the outward forms of saintliness, wisdom, kindness and morality; for as the *Tao Te Ching* says:

> These three are outward forms alone;
> they are not sufficient in themselves.
> It is more important
> To see the simplicity
> To realize one's true nature
> To cast off selfishness
> And temper desire.[7]

Wisdom, kindness, and morality if they are assumed by man in their outward forms are didactic and inclined to tell people what to *do;* as they become interiorized in the sage, so he is enabled to demonstrate what they are not by teaching them but by living them.

Guénon's deliberate search for impersonality was in pursuance of this ideal. He had found, by means of symbolic language, his contact with Principial Truth and he lived it according to his own individual personal situation and needs. Others to whom the teaching can reveal the Truth will be in a position to do likewise. What practical steps have to be taken to engage in the search will naturally vary from person to person. Once the principle of the symbolic nature of the phenomenal world has been grasped, the practical realization of what is implicit in this knowledge will gradually (i.e., step by step) become evident. Like John Henry Newman, we no longer ask to see the distant scene but are content to take the next step in faith.

This process in its general aspect can be described as the re-sacralization of the universe, the restoration of 'meaning to life in all its aspects and activities, above and beyond scientific materialism and practical utility. This re-sacralization can and should begin with the simplest and the most mundane aspects of our lives on a daily basis: awakening from sleep as a resurrection from death and darkness; washing as a physical *and* spiritual symbol of purification and the restoration to a state of primal simplicity and innocence; the breaking of the fast seen as the maintenance of physical strength through

---

7. *Tao Te Ching,* chap. 19.

participation in the strength of the natural world, which we incorporate and make our own; the rhythm of action and inaction seen as reproducing the rhythm of all life which, if we are aware, will teach us to 'live that we may dread the grave as little as our bed.' Thus a single day epitomizes an individual life, and an individual life span symbolizes the total span of manifest existence.

The difficulty many will experience in taking seriously such suggestions will indicate how far we have departed from living a balanced life as it should naturally and spontaneously be lived. But if we stop and reverse, even in the slightest degree, the onrush of materialistic 'explanations' and the ensuing impoverishment of the quality of our lives, then we shall be able to create for ourselves an openness, a space, in which the *Atman* can be discovered. If we allow our common everyday language to be heard attentively we shall truthfully be able to say 'We are getting to the heart of the matter,' and words as simple and familiar as those of the old hymn will take on a new and deeper meaning and relevance:

> Blest are the pure in heart
> For they shall see our God
> The secret of the Lord is theirs
> Their Soul is Christ's abode.

> Still to the lowly soul
> He doth himself impart
> And for his dwelling and his throne
> Chooseth the pure in heart.

We in the West are called upon to discover from the ruins of our past those insights which are needed to reconstruct and restore 'continuity of life', *solve et coagula*. Guénon was convinced that the Roman Catholic Church was the vehicle for the West to convey the one tradition, and therefore it is the most natural place at which to begin our search, at least for the majority. But to quote Coleridge once again: 'He who begins by loving Christianity better than Truth will proceed by loving his own Sect or Church better than Christianity and end in loving himself better than all.' Or as Eckhart says: 'To seek God by rituals is to get the ritual and lose God in the process.'

6

IN SEARCH OF THE LOST WORD

INITIATION AND SPIRITUAL GROWTH

We should never cease to behave and to think as if the Unknowable was capable of being known, even if we know that it is infinite and beyond our grasp.

MAETERLINCK

SOME FIFTY-FIVE YEARS AGO certain philosophical circles in France made use of a common French word in a rather specialized way. The word is *dépassement,* and one of its users defined it thus:

> It signifies the opening of thought to an evolving universe which is not confined either to a permanent established system such as scholasticism nor to a mechanistic materialism, nor to a purely scientific viewpoint, e.g., neo-positivism, but which aims at embracing the totality of the world, physical and spiritual.[1]

This particular work is concerned with the ideas of Teilhard de Chardin, a thinker not esteemed very highly by Guénon, who was by nature unlikely to concede much importance to Teilhard's mixture of mysticism and profane science. But the notion of *dépassement,* a sense of the unity underlying all that is, and the existence of an invisible spiritual world of which the manifest world is in some

1. F. A. Viallet, *Le Dépassement* (Paris, 1961).

way symbolic and on which it depends, is as old as mankind itself and has never been abandoned, even in the West, though here it has been almost obliterated.

Given such a universal longing among the members of the human race, what are the means by which it can be satisfied? It can only be satisfied by the establishment of personal and collective links with this Ultimate Reality, and this is the objective of initiation in all its aspects.

Initiation, in whatever form it may appear, is that which really incarnates the 'spirit' of a tradition, and is also that which allows of the effective realization of 'supra-human' states.[2]

As Guénon pointed out, all initiation is operative, not speculative. For members of traditional societies, initiation was an absolute *sine qua non* of their existence; without it they literally could not go on living a satisfactory life. It was for them the spiritual complement of growth towards physical maturity. Birth and death were the fundamental symbols of all initiatory experience. The basic concepts were those of spiritual birth and of death and resurrection to new life, and this was as essential and as natural a part of human life as was physical change. Life was inconceivable without it, and where it was not available for any reason, those who suffered such deprivation found life precarious and meaningless.

Western civilization is deficient in this respect as in so many others. All the authentic channels of initiatory experience have become silted up and only the faintest trickle finds its way into modern life. Initiation has two main aspects, personal and social; its objective is always spiritual growth and final deliverance from illusion. In practical terms, it provides a framework and a timetable for the ordering of the individual's life. Men and women were once familiar with such concepts as the seven ages of man. Each period of a life was defined and had appropriate duties and responsibilities and from each period appropriate achievements were expected. Thus initiation can be compared to what anthropologists have called *rites de passage*. Initiation is not only a door through which

---

2. Guénon, *The Reign of Quantity,* chap. 28.

one passes, but in the rites and teaching connected with the passage from one state to another there is, as Guénon says, a powerful preservation of traditional teaching and action.

Perhaps two examples, from the many which could be chosen, of the West's failure to provide any kind of valid initiatory experience may be mentioned here. In the spiritual sphere, the Christian Church has entirely lost the 'inwardness' of its initiatory practices. The initiatory symbolism attached to the rite of baptism is now forgotten, and hence neglected and only faintly suspected by the vast majority, for whom baptism is little more than a convenient occasion for the registration of personal names. The rites attending death are similarly misunderstood or neglected; the result being that the concept of death as *mors janua vitae* has been replaced by the obscene efforts of profane medicine to prolong life at the biological level only, which is one more example of the utter confusion in which we find ourselves, dominated by the reign of quantity at the expense of quality, of matter over spirit.

One example of the social aspect of initiation must suffice. In traditional societies, in which work was not merely a 'secular' occupation but an important part of one's personal spiritual development, initiation included initiation into one's *métier,* into the 'craft and mystery' of the various necessary trades and professions. Such occupations were seen as contributions to the maintenance of the fabric of creation and the preservation of its harmony and balance; even more than that, they were felt to be participation in the creative activity of the supreme power always at work in the world. Specialized groups naturally enough developed their own forms of initiation based on an appropriate craft symbolism. All the necessary arts were included: healing, protecting (warriors), building, fishing and hunting, cultivating the soil, and a host of others, as civilizations became more complicated.

What is left of these vital means of initiation? Virtually nothing. In England there are the city guilds, now totally profane; in France they have the last relics of the same in *compagnonnage;* and throughout the world there is Freemasonry, which has now lost all links with its operative aspects while retaining some of its value as an initiatory organization.

The disappearance of this framework for life has resulted in much distress and unhappiness at every level, including the degradation of work and its complete secularization, and the definition of its value in predominantly monetary terms. One result of this is the rise of closely knit, anti-social, adolescent groups or gangs and a host of sub-cultures more or less completely estranged from the mainstream and from one another. Gangs of all sorts, in default of society doing so, provide young people with a definition of adulthood, initiatory tests, special names or totems, passwords, and a secret language, powerful inner cohesion and severe sanctions for failure to conform. They are in fact a parody of a real initiatory organization since they lack the one thing essential for any genuine initiatory group; namely, an authentic teaching derived from a valid tradition handed down by qualified teachers.

Initiation thus facilitates the passage of men and women through the various stages of their earthly pilgrimage by the valid transmission of authentic knowledge—what Guénon calls 'spiritual influence'. In conformity with his choice of Advaita Vedanta as the vehicle for the transmission of traditional teaching, he avoids any hint of anthropomorphic symbolism in his references to the Ultimate Reality. As Jean Servier has said:

> To know is to be.... Initiation alone can provide the knowledge, which is an awareness of being. Knowledge is primarily tradition.... By knowledge the initiate is brought into the presence of being, which is a homogeneous continuum, invisible but present throughout the phenomenal world. He learns to see objects not as something over against him, but rather what is nevertheless fixed; like an actor in a play, who can add some stage business and *ad lib* replies, provided that he does his best to interpret the author's intentions. So initiation among other things gives the initiate a global vision of the world.[3]

As we ponder the themes of initiation, one unchanging belief emerges, namely, that the initiative is always with the Invisible, which chooses its own: 'You have not chosen me. I have chosen you.'

---

3. J. Servier, *L'Homme et l'Invisible* (Paris, 1980), pp105–6.

Thus all initiatory activity is response to a prior calling. This power is called by Guénon *la volonté supérieure,* the higher will. This is not exactly equivalent to the Christian 'will of God', but nearer the pre-Christian Stoic concept of a non-personal divinity which pervades the world and leads all things, including man, to their final destiny. Such a will should not be conceived of as possessing such human characteristics as benevolence, but at least it can be considered as beneficent in that it draws man towards the truth he was destined to seek.

The place of initiation in the modern world has been taken by what we now call 'education', a most unsatisfactory substitute. Varro, the great Latin polymath, underlines the fact that *educo* is primarily concerned with the material aspects of child rearing: *educit obstetrix, educat nutrix, instituit paedagogus, docet magister.*[4] The midwife and the nurse educate, the pedagogue institutes and instructs, the master teaches (*docet,* from the Zend root *da,* 'to know'). True teaching is the imparting of knowledge, and know-ledge is, in traditional societies, primarily knowledge of the spiritual. Other knowledge there is, and this must be acquired; but it only makes sense and can only be purposefully used when it is related to the underlying spiritual knowledge.

The substance of all initiatory training is the transmission of this spiritual knowledge, which is supernatural in origin and alone satisfies man's desire for *dépassement* or transcendence. This traditional learning is universal in its dissemination and in its application; it is not primarily religious in the limited sense of that word as being the prerogative of any individual religious organization, but is what all authentic religious traditions have in common. The distinctive differences of these traditions are in fact only different ways of embodying and realizing this primary truth, each religion at this point in time having a separate and unique contribution to make towards the full comprehension of Ultimate Reality.

The Primordial Tradition underlies and validates all the different 'technical' aspects of initiation and is the key to their understanding. These cover two essential aspects of any individual's life, his life as a

---

4. Lewis and Short, *Latin Dictionary,* 'educo'.

separate sentient being, unique in essence, and his life as a member of a family, a group, a city or town, a tribe or nation, and of the world.

The personal need for initiation was never divorced from the social aspect until recently in the West, when the spheres of the sacred and the profane were felt to be in opposition, even hostile, to one another. It is this union, in which all aspects of life are seen as sacred, that provides initiation with its language—the language of symbols, which has been elaborated over the centuries. Starting with himself, man finds his body provides a fund of symbols: the heart, the lungs, the bowels, the reproductive organs—all have a part in the language of symbols, as does every aspect of the world around him. But equally, man's activities are all regulated by an ideal and eternal counterpart. Hence the evolution of ritual acts, carrying a weight of meaning far beyond what we can easily comprehend in the modern world. The elaboration of ritual acts, from those that mimic the natural effect desired, to the most complex religious rite with many layers of meaning, are all part of what has to be learnt, and are also in themselves and their performance part of initiation. They follow the cycle of the seasons and draw from them deep symbolic meanings and analogies. The main elements of initiation, as we have seen, are all related: death and resurrection, the second birth, the journey with its stages and tests, all tell of the same transformation ending in deliverance and union.

Traditional societies have a very high doctrine of man, destined by the supreme power to be manifested and reintegrated, and to pass through a period when he is dominated by the illusion of separation which is dispelled in the *waḥdat al-wujūd* of Islamic Sufism. This high calling of man is explained by St Augustine who said: 'God became man in order that man might become God.' This is also seen as the restoration in every man of the Primordial perfect Adam. Initiatic teaching explains to man his place in the hierarchy of being: 'Created a little lower than the angels but crowned with glory and honor.'

All traditional teaching is oral; the spoken word alone is authentic, for was it not by the speaking of God that all things came into being? The notion of harmony is derived from the harmony of sounds, which have a deep symbolic significance and speak to us at a more profound level than any of the other senses. The natural sounds that surround us have a potency and meaning stronger than perceptions by any other of the senses. Allied to this sense of the supreme importance of sound is its correlation with rhythmic movements of all kinds, through which catharsis can be achieved of all pent-up emotion. This emotion is never wasted, but by dance and music is transformed into the means of entry into a new and qualitatively higher sphere of existence.

The spoken word is crucial to all initiation. It was enunciated by the teacher and absorbed and interiorized by the pupil, who was given his own personal *mantra* or form of words, which by its sound reflected and reinforced its meaning. The frequent repetition of sacred phrases is what Guénon calls incantation, which he distinguishes from the Christian notion of petitionary prayer. In an important passage he describes it thus:

> The incantation thus defined as an entirely inward operation in principle can nonetheless in many cases be expressed and 'supported' outwardly by words or gestures that constitute initiatic rites, such as the *mantra* in the Hindu tradition or the *dhikr* in the Islamic tradition, which must be thought of as producing rhythmic vibrations that reverberate throughout a more or less extensive domain in the indefinite series of the states of the being. Whether the result obtained be more or less complete, the final goal is always the realization in oneself of 'Universal Man' by the perfect communion of all these states in proper and harmonious hierarchy and in an integral expansion, both in 'amplitude' and 'exaltation', that is, both as to the horizontal expansion of the modalities of each state and the vertical superposition of the different states, according to the geometrical figuration that we have explained in detail elsewhere.[5]

Guénon emphasized the existence of various stages in the initiatic process and in this follows the Islamic distinctions between the different stages. The first stage, which in Arabic is called *'ilm al-yaqīn*, is

---

5. Guénon, *Perspectives on Initiation*, chap. 24.

the stage of the simple believer who believes in a personalized external reality, God, to whom he can relate by means of the performance of religious rituals and petitionary prayer. This is the state of many who are satisfied with the exoteric aspects of their religion and for whom dogma and doctrine are all-important. The second, known as *'ayn al-yaqīn*, refers to the ecstatic or 'out-of-the-person' experience of the initiate. This implies realization of the possibility of the third state without actually experiencing it, except passively and, as it were, by its imposition from outside. The third state, the *ḥaqq al-yaqīn*, is the highest possible experience available to men, that of consciously willed complete realization in all modalities, physical, psychical and spiritual, of the Universal Man united to the source of illumination in a complete identification in which the Source and its recipient cease to be separate. This 'high' doctrine of man has ceased to be treated as a practical possibility in the West, and St Paul's 'I live yet not I but Christ lives in me' is usually considered an example of his hyperbole and not a practical goal for ordinary people. And yet the purpose of all initiation is the attainment of the realization in his or her own being of the total possibilities of the Universal Man embracing all mankind in its possibility of perfection. Few in the West can conceive that such an experience of total irreversible union is possible.

In the West such initiatory stages have been limited to the psychic realm. Many have thought that Jungian depth psychology is the 'modern' equivalent of initiation in traditional societies. In Guénon's view nothing could be further from the truth. The psychic realm, lying as it does between the corporeal and the spiritual, is nevertheless part of the realm of manifestation and can never be the locus of true spiritual initiation. Not only is this so, but depth psychology opens the way for lower psychic influences to gain dominance and often results in the parodying of real initiation and the blocking of any true spiritual development towards the goal of spiritual deliverance.

Once again we find ourselves deprived of all those human supports with which we are accustomed to comfort ourselves and are faced with Guénon's relentless 'Not this, not this.' As he pointed out, initiation is not something added on to profane education, nor a higher form of it; nor is it the antithesis of it. It is not a separate philosophical system nor is it a specialized science. It is none of these things because it is of a totally different order and thus cannot be compared with anything on the profane level, nor can the terms used to describe it be derived from anything on that level.

Perhaps the word 'teaching' is misleading. Initiation might better be described as assistance rendered to the pupil, enabling him or her to cultivate a different way of seeing things. That is to say, seeing what the profane eye sees, but drawing totally different conclusions from it, seeing also what is invisible to the profane eye; the difference between seeing in a glass darkly and seeing face to face. The cultivation, in other words, of a power of apprehension unknown and undesired by those whose vision and interest are restricted to the material world 'of ten thousand things', to use a Taoist phrase.

Initiation has sometimes been described as the drawing aside of a curtain. In our everyday language we frequently equate seeing with understanding, thereby implicitly referring to the deep symbolic significance of sight and sight opposed to blindness and the dark, and their final resolution in the primal unity in which darkness and sight are both alike. Sense metaphors lead us beyond the senses, and whether we hear or see or taste or grasp, what we apprehend is what Jesus referred to when he called upon those who had ears to hear, to hear: the spiritual meaning of his message.

Initiatory organizations of all kinds have frequently been accused of being secret societies or of purveying some secret learning, but this is to misunderstand the true nature of the 'secret'. What is transmitted by initiation is not some secret formulae, nor a series of secret rites and ceremonies, nor passwords or secret signs of recognition; all these are far from being the message itself. The message is, by definition, incommunicable in words and is only heard by him that hath ears to hear the unspoken, to see the invisible, and to grasp the incomprehensible. 'The Tao that can be told is not the eternal Tao. The name that can be named is not the eternal name'; so this incommunicability is part of its very nature. Because this is so, and because the quest in which initiates are engaged is sacred in character, reserve and discretion are essential. In the West there is a perverted belief that everything should be available to everybody, and that what cannot be described in language understandable by a schoolboy, or a subscriber to *The Reader's Digest*, is probably pretentious nonsense—unless, that is, it is 'scientific', in which case it is accepted with reverent awe and accorded respect *because* it is not understood. All notions of hierarchy and human distinctions have been obscured and derided and a person's true place in society remains a mystery. Part of Guénon's answer to this problem he found in the caste system which, whatever the defects of its practical outwork in present-day India, is nevertheless a truthful antidote to evolutionary democracy and the belief in ever-increasing progress on the material and intellectual level. True initiatory teaching recognizes the various levels of capability, the essential dignity of all men and the value of every task in the maintenance of cosmic harmony. Gandhi's insistence on the sharing of so-called menial and degrading tasks by everyone is a better answer to the problem of differentials than the politics of envy and 'every man for himself' which prevails so widely today.

One initiatic organization in which Guénon was greatly interested throughout his life and about which he wrote a great deal was Freemasonry. One might have imagined that Guénon would have dismissed it as one more man-made hotchpotch of various occult and hermetic traditions without value or importance. The fact that he did not do so compels us to take it seriously.

For Guénon, Freemasonry was the receptacle of a vast fund of traditional wisdom, particularly rich in initiatory symbolism and rituals. He was convinced that Masonry had been the means whereby many aspects of Christianity, which had been lost or neglected over the course of time, had been preserved. As Christianity became more and more dogmatic, institutionalized, and exoteric in its Western form, so the esoteric aspects, so necessary for its inner spiritual life, became diminished and pushed out onto the fringe, and accusations of heresy became the means of suppressing that essential freedom without which any organization ceases to develop. Such minority groups, Guénon firmly believed, found their refuge in Freemasonry. The two groups who contributed most in this way were the Templars, whose suppression in 1314 marked a turning point in the spiritual history of Europe, and the Rosicrucians, who, when they retired to the East, left many of their secrets with the Masons.

Orthodox historical methods will deny outright such insubstantial claims, in much the same way that certain critical attacks have denied almost every fact of Christian history. The historical method desacralizes everything it touches. Guénon was very cavalier in his treatment of profane historians who have deemed his case unproven. The vast majority of Freemasons go along with the profane view and many Anglo-Saxon Masons are unaware of the existence of the higher grades in whose rituals and teaching the bulk of this symbolic initiatory teaching is contained. But in France there are a few influential figures who, although not agreeing with all that Guénon wrote, nevertheless recognize that he was a powerful voice recalling the order to its spiritual vocation and reminding it of the vast store of traditional wisdom enshrined in its teaching. In Guénon's view the exact historical means whereby this store was accumulated and transmitted is not nearly as important as the fact that it exists and corresponds with the other traditions making up the sum of the Primordial Tradition. While he firmly maintained the antiquity and authenticity of the majority of Masonic teaching, Guénon did not hesitate to point out certain later accretions which were not in conformity with tradition, notably ideas derived from eighteenth-century illuminism introduced into Masonry by Dom Pernety, who had in turn been influenced by Swedenborg. Another importation of a later date connected with the Theosophical movement was the notion of *supéreurs inconnus*, the unknown masters, in whose hands lay the destiny of the world and from whom the leaders of the movement received their orders. In Guénon's view these and other aberrations did not, however, invalidate the bulk of Masonic teaching. These and other related matters are, as Guénon said, 'extremely complex' and detailed discussion of them lies outside the scope of this book. Perhaps, however, Masons dissatisfied with the low spiritual level of their lodges will look again at Guénon's ideas and work towards the recovery of *la parole perdue* and all that is embodied in that phrase.

Christians should also be more open to discovering the hidden riches of Masonic teaching, and openness and interchange of ideas between Masons and Christians should be promoted in English-speaking Masonry, as it already is on the continent. On the face of it, Guénon's contribution to French Freemasonry may seem negligible, since only a minority group comprising *La Grande Loge Nationale Française* takes him seriously, and the Lodge founded to study his work, *The Great Triad,* was short lived. But Guénon did not seek the approval of the majority, and enunciated facts and principles that are of universal and unchanging value—the 'landmarks' of Masonry. In so doing he reopened a door long closed and reminded Masons of the true initiatory nature and function of their brotherhood.

7

A PRIEST FOREVER AFTER THE ORDER OF MELCHIZEDEK

THE MOMENT OF VISION

He who knows both knowledge and action, with action overcomes death and with knowledge reaches immortality.

Into deep darkness fall those who follow the immanent. Into deeper darkness fall those who follow the transcendent.

One is the outcome of the transcendent and another is the outcome of the immanent. Thus have we heard from the ancient sages who explained this truth to us.

He who knows both the transcendent and the immanent, with the immanent overcomes death and with the transcendent reaches immortality.

The face of truth remains hidden behind a circle of gold, unveil it, oh god of light, that I who love the true, may see!

Oh life-giving sun, offspring of the Lord of Creation, solitary seer of Heaven! spread thy light and withdraw thy blinding splendor that I may behold thy radiant form: that Spirit far away within thee, is my own inmost Spirit.

Isa Upanishad, tr. J. Mascaro, in the Penguin edition of the *Bhagavad Gita*, p18.

SOMEWHERE in all our studying and reading there must come that moment which is the moment of vision; the moment of purest joy in which we know that we are part of the balanced and harmonious unity of the all. Once we know this, we are unshakable and can, as Clement of Alexandria said, 'faultlessly play to the end the part in the drama of life for which God has cast us.' This, the playful calm of the sage, is the *ur-grund* of all true religion as well as its supreme objective, the Beatific Vision, deliverance from illusion and partiality, moksa, call it what you will.

The various world religions have until now seemed to be mutually exclusive and often in opposition to one another. Now we are beginning to understand that they are complementary, like the individual colors of the spectrum, each distinct and unique and yet all needed to make up the pure white light of truth.

Guénon always insisted that adherence to and the practice of one of these great religions was essential for everyone. For most of us in the West we still adhere to Christianity, or Judaism or Islam, the three great monotheistic religions. It is among these three closely related expressions of the tradition that we can most naturally begin our search for reconciliation and better understanding by means of inter-faith dialogue. This is so, in spite of the fact that our common origin has until now been as much a stumbling block as a help to mutual understanding. Members of a family, if they fall out, often find it more difficult to come together again than they do to be reconciled with total strangers.

The separations between Jew, Christian, and Muslim are still close and painful, there are wounds as yet unhealed; the Crucifixion, anti-Semitism and the Crusades are still living issues. Nevertheless, the path to better understanding is open to us and more and more fruitful explorations are being made. Guénon himself opened up a perspective that could prove to be valuable in promoting mutual understanding. He has suggested that the mysterious figure of Melchizedek, the priest-king of Salem, may furnish a common point of reference from which to begin.

It has frequently been said that the three religions have a common ancestor in the person of Abraham, the first Muslim and founder of the Jewish people. But if we look closely at the narrative of the Old

Testament, we find that the position of Abraham lies midway in the story of man's relationship with God and is not its beginning. He is situated halfway between the first covenant between God and Adam (Eccles. 17:12) and the Mosaic covenant on Mount Sinai. Before Abraham came the covenant with Noah (Gen. 9:8–17) which, as Professor C.H. Dodd says, 'stands as a witness that God's covenant, though historically it was made with Israel, is applicable to the whole human race.'[1] Between Adam and Noah came the covenant between God and Adam's third son, Seth (Gen. 4:26), and finally came the Mosaic covenant, which defined the Jewish people as chosen for a special purpose.

We need to remember, however, that all these covenants were not exclusive but were intended to embrace all men, or better, to show that all men are in a covenanted relationship with the Eternal. Robert Aron puts it well when he says:

> The Covenant is not an isolated fact in the history of God or in the human tradition.... Covenant is written into us, it is a permanent part of our being. Wherever a man thinks of God, whether to pledge Him allegiance or to oppose Him, with doubt or refusal, wherever a man or a group of men face the insoluble problem, wherever there is a dialogue concerned with the paradox of God's insertion in history, of man and the insertion of man in eternity, the Covenant goes on and is renewed. This Covenant set up just as the biblical faith was beginning to develop, cannot be broken by either disbelief or bigotry. It endures even when men fall away from God or attempt to draw too close to Him, whether they abandon His worship or conduct it with the empty formalism and exclusiveness of which God showed his disapproval at the end of the Flood. The Covenant is consubstantial with man, in as much as he is a man, just as it is necessary to God because He is God. It is the permanent and universal woof of the living history of God and of the history of mankind.[2]

---

1. C.H. Dodd, *The Bible Today* (n.d.), p114.
2. R. Aron, *The God of the Beginnings* (NY, 1966), pp103–4.

This is entirely consistent with Guénon's teaching and is another way of understanding the Primordial Tradition, which is, as it were, ratified by the historical covenants. Israel misunderstood the nature of the covenant during the formative period of its development as a nation, but later the prophets recovered the original universal intention of God's covenant with Israel.

The person of Melchizedek can provide us with a starting point. The references to him in the Bible, though quite infrequent, are intriguing. In Genesis 14 we read of a strange encounter which took place in 'the King's dale.' Abraham was resting there after defeating the enemies of his nephew Lot. While so doing he was visited and greeted by 'Melchizedek King of Salem', who brought forth bread and wine and was the Priest of the most high God, and he said 'Blessed be Abraham of the most high God, possessor of heaven and earth... and he [Abraham] gave him tithes of all.' At first sight this seems to be one of many strange and inexplicable incidents recorded in the Old Testament. But as we shall see, it had for the writers of both the Old and the New Testaments great significance, as it did for Jesus also.

Melchizedek seems to have naturally assumed precedence over Abraham and to have been both king and priest and worthy of receiving homage in the form of tithes from him. His offering of bread and wine is unusual and, as Guénon points out, bread and wine are universally connected with initiation ceremonies. What was happening? Guénon in his chapter on Melchizedek in *The King of the World*, remarks:

> Wine is often taken to represent the authentic initiatic tradition...; the use of wine in a rite confers upon that rite a clearly initiatic character; such is the case notably of the 'eucharistic' sacrifice of Melchizedek.[3]

Guénon goes on then to elucidate the universality of Melchizedek as the lawgiver and priest, as well as his counterparts in other traditions, notably Manu in the Vedic tradition. Jean Tourniac, in his book on Melchizedek, says flatly that Melchizedek *is* the Primordial

3. Guénon, *The King of the World* chap 6.

Tradition.[4] He unites in his person regal and priestly functions and is the true source of justice

> in both the strictest and the most complete sense of the word, implying essentially the idea of balance or harmony and indissolubly linked with 'Peace'.[5]

Melchizedek appears again later on in the great messianic Psalm 110, which is unparalleled in the whole Psalter as a prophecy foretelling the coming of the Messiah, of whom, as the psalm says in verse four, 'The Lord swore and will not repent: thou art a priest for ever after the order of Melchizedek.' Jesus himself commented on this psalm (Mark 12:36; Luke 20:42), and St Peter uses it in his sermon on the day of Pentecost (Acts 2:34). The author of the Epistle to the Hebrews also develops the idea of the eternally-valid King-Priest, the Messiah, the Holy One of God, thereby confirming the eternal, universal, and supernatural covenant of God with men revealed in the person of Jesus. Thus the earthly Mosaic covenant of Sinai is no longer to be exclusive, temporal, and nationalistic but is revealed to be eternal, inclusive of all men, and spiritual in nature. It was St Augustine who declared that 'the Christian religion has always been in the world; only after the coming of Christ was it called Christianity.'[6]

Traditional teaching has always made much of sacred sites, and in the sacred topography of the Judeo-Christian tradition Jerusalem has always been the center. Today it is the holy city of Jew, Christian and Muslim and is traditionally associated with Melchizedek's Salem, originally said to have been located on Mount Moriah where Abraham prepared to sacrifice Isaac. Under David the city came into Jewish hands and was made the center of religious and royal life. No other city in the world can be compared with it. It is the earthly counterpart of that eternal city, 'the Jerusalem which is above is free; the mother of us all' (Gal. 4:26). This ideal Jerusalem is linked with the renewal of the eternal covenant through the Christ and

---

4. J. Tourniac, *Melkitsedeq ou la Tradition Primordiale* (Paris, 1983).
5. Guénon, *The King of the World,* chap. 6.
6. St Augustine, *Opera* (1598); cf. *In Joan. Evang.,* CVI, 4.

contrasted with the temporal covenant of Mount Sinai which bears children for slavery (Gal. 4:25).

For the modern profane world such speculations are superfluous; the need is for economic, social and political action. Many, however, will echo the belief expressed by a Muslim writer in a symposium on Muslim-Christian relationships:

> There can be no settlement of the Palestinian question by force or by practical means; it will only be settled when representatives of the three great religions, for whom Jerusalem is a holy city, can pray there together for peace.[7]

Other situations will remain equally intractable until their spiritual dimension is recognized and given priority.

Melchizedek and his holy city Jerusalem can together form a starting point from which Jew, Christian, and Muslim could retrace their steps and discover how they became separated and hostile to one another. It is worth pointing out the important part that Melchizedek plays in Shi'ite gnosticism, in which he is identified with the twelfth Imam, the *Imām qā'im*, the hidden Imam who is to reappear at the end of time. The ramifications of this important fact have been described at length for Western readers by Henri Corbin in his four-volume work *En Islam iranien*, where many striking analogies and confirmations of the teaching of the Primordial Tradition, as expounded by Guénon, can be found.

I hope some indication has been given of the possible areas into which scholars and people of goodwill might move. This will perforce be largely the work of an élite with the necessary spiritual insights and scholarly qualifications. But all of us may in our various ways move out of our exclusive attitudes and see in other religions the fresh insights given to them by the one indivisible spirit.

Another area of exploration are the Traditional Sciences, among which is the science of Sacred Numbers. For a long time now numerology has been the preserve of the lunatic fringe and has allowed fanatics of various kinds to prove their particular points with great

---

7. *Verse et Controverse*: *Le Chrétien en dialogue avec le Monde,* 14, 'Les Musulmans' (Paris, 1971), p134.

ingenuity but with almost total ignorance of the princi-ples underlying the right use of numbers. Little has appeared in English of any real worth, but in French the works of Matila Ghyka and Dr René Allendy are of great importance.[8] Guénon himself, since he was a mathematician by training, naturally paid a great deal of attention to this subject, notably in two of his later published works, *The Metaphysical Principles of the Infinitesimal Calculus* and *The Great Triad*. In the preface to the former Guénon states his view uncompromisingly:

> We have often pointed out that most profane sciences, even when they still to some degree are related to reality, only represent the dregs of these sciences. Because they have lost all connection with underlying principles and have followed a course of independent development, they have come to be regarded as a self-authenticating body of knowledge, whereas in fact, for precisely this reason, they have practically ceased to have any value at all.

In *The Great Triad* he expounds the ternary nature of the old Chinese conception of Earth, Man, and Heaven and its analogies in many other forms of the tradition. Vast areas of study remain to be covered in this field, as in many others. As an example of the way in which a reconsideration of numbers is valuable, I will quote a passage from Dr Allendy's book:

> We can interpret the number 12 as the sum of 10 + 2, as the idea of the integral unity of the universe, associated with the idea of differentiation—since the number 2 represents the idea of Differentiation as such, i.e., as a pure abstraction on the metaphysical plane, and that the number 20 (10 x 2) represents Differentiation governing the Universe, embracing the totality of the Universe and dividing it into two opposing polarities. The number 12 should be understood as the figuration of the Universe in the plenitude of its unity, but envisaged from the point of view of differentiation, i.e. the Universe as containing a binary polarity,

---

8. Matila Ghyka, *Le Nombre d'Or* (Paris, 1959; 1982).

which gives it its structure and orientation. Thus the antagonistic forces of creation (binary) find their locus of application on the Cosmos as a unit and in so doing realize the structure (1 + 2 = 3). Care should be taken to emphasize the difference between the idea of a Duality which divides the Universe into two opposing camps: Good and Evil, Life and Death (an idea expressed by the number 20) and the idea of a Universe which is truly a unity, but containing within that unity a structure and differentiation (an idea expressed by the number 12).[9]

Many readers will find this perplexing. It is helpful, perhaps, to involve the imagination and treat the passage like a poem. Insight into the underlying symbolic logic may also be found in the ideas of Jung and his followers, e.g., Marie Louise Franz, who has pointed out the difficulty:

> The great problem posed by the application of natural numbers to the understanding of synchronistic phenomena is as already mentioned the fact that a *qualitative* aspect [my emphasis] must be attributed to them.[10]

This qualitative aspect of numbers is one which modern mathematicians have almost forgotten but is now being recovered via depth psychology. Many other suggestions could be made as to where and how one could begin the journey home. But prescriptive suggestions defeat their own purpose. Everyone by the use of his or her imagination and insight will find what is appropriate for them.

> Seeing the small is insight
> Yielding to force is strength
> Using the outer light, return to insight,
> And in this way be saved from harm.
> This is learning constancy.[11]

---

9. René Allendy, *Le Symbolisme des Nombres* (Paris, 1948; reprinted 1984), p 327.
10. M.L. von Franz, *Number and Time* (1974), p 59.
11. *Tao Te Ching*, chap. 52.

8

CHRIST AND COSMOS

THE RABBI OF NAZARETH & HIS TEACHING

In the previous chapter we have suggested some ways in which progress towards unity may come about and certain areas for possible reconciliation. In this chapter I wish to be more specific about the task which faces the Christian Church in the West as the authentic vehicle for the transmission of the Primordial Tradition.

Guénon never faltered in his belief that the Catholic Church was an authentic transmitter of Tradition, but he frequently lamented the extent to which it had deviated from the path of Tradition, thus emphasizing the magnitude of the task confronting those who wished to return to the true way.

The task before us takes on two aspects. Firstly, that of diagnosing the true seriousness and extent of our deviation from the Truth; secondly, the possible paths to recovery that lie before us. These have already been discussed in general terms. But if, as Guénon believed, the Christian Church holds a special position in the West comparable to that held by the great religious traditions of the East, then it is imperative that an attempt should be made to clarify what needs to be done and how it can be done.

Following Guénon's approach it would seem essential that we should first carefully follow Guénon's diagnosis of our ills. In order to do this we must go back to the first enunciation of the Way for the West in the life and teaching of Jesus, and ask ourselves how it has come about that his teaching—which told us that the Truth will make us free and that if Jesus makes us free, we shall be free indeed (John 8:32, 36)—has resulted in the emergence of an institution which, over the centuries, has perpetrated a vast range of oppressive acts and has fostered fanaticism, bigotry and persecution in the name of its founder.

Such an enquiry has been undertaken many times before; indeed, it may be said to be a persistent feature of the life of the Church and that it is this self-critical dissatisfaction that has enabled the Church to survive, however precariously and with ever-diminishing efficacy, up to the present time. One could go further and say that it is this awareness of the historical element in the Church's life and of the inevitability of change which is the distinctive characteristic of the presentation of the Tradition in the West.

All human institutions follow certain inexorable paths, through an initial period of creation and direct inspiration from the founder, into a period of expansion and dilution during which the original freedom and inspiration, based on personal oral teaching by the founder, gives way to interpretation, systematization and written expression. Finally there is what Guénon calls a process of 'solidification' in which dogma rules and orthodoxy is the most sought after virtue. Following this is what Guénon calls the stage of 'dissolution' in which all previous certainties are dissolved and there is no consensus of belief; sects proliferate, and chaos ensues. The defenders of orthodoxy retreat behind their prepared lines of defense, the majority of the faithful is left leaderless and confused, and the remainder follows an unending variety of personal opinions, for the most part far removed from any authentic traditional wisdom. Secular institutions that outlive their usefulness decay and are replaced by others. In the case of the Church, which owes its origin to supra-human inspiration, there is always the possibility of re-creation from within by a rediscovery of the original inspiration. It seems that a critical point in the process of decay and dissolution has to be reached before this can come about. This point seems to have been reached in the West and the process of restoration can begin, providing that there are sufficient numbers of people with enough courage and insight to undertake the task.

Even the most cursory examination will reveal how the teaching of Jesus was perverted and manipulated by the Church, and how we can now, after two millennia, begin to rectify these mistakes. Many of the most creative individuals seeking spiritual regeneration and the re-sacralization of the cosmos will be found outside the confines of the Church or adhering to other religious traditions. This is a fundamental prerequisite for success, for the enterprise must not be confined to those who 'profess and call themselves Christians'. We recall Jesus' saying, 'Not everyone that saith unto me Lord, Lord, shall enter into the Kingdom of heaven, but he that doeth the will of my Father which is in heaven' (Matt. 7:21). With this open and inclusive attitude must go a willingness to accept the validity and authenticity of the deposit of truth in other religious faiths and a firm conviction that the 'spiritual influences' have been genuinely guiding them. All exclusiveness and triumphalism must be abandoned by Christians; claims to be the sole deposit of truth are irrelevant, unprovable and contrary to the spirit of Jesus' teaching. Equally, all facile attempts to seek a lowest common denominator or a statement of faith on which all can agree are just as much to be avoided. What is essential is an open-minded expectant willingness to listen to what other religious traditions are saying to us and to consider what insights we can receive from them to enlighten our own understanding.

To achieve this humble listening attitude a *metanoia is* essential—a total reorientation of one's whole being by means of a renewed commitment to living the truth at no matter what cost, including a willingness to discard all that one has hitherto considered irreplaceable in one's religious life. This is not a willed rejection of past attitudes but a natural growth from one state to another, with its own pace and inherent nature, which we cannot control by reason or will but which we can and should assent to and welcome.

Understanding our past will help us to rectify our present condition and enable Christianity to recover its credibility as a vehicle of spiritual truth. Why did the message of freedom proclaimed by Jesus become an instrument of state policy for the maintenance of the crumbling Roman Empire? Can we now agree with John Stuart Mill that 'it is one of the most tragic facts of all history that Constantine rather than Marcus Aurelius was the first Christian Emperor'? How far Constantine was personally to blame for what happened and how far it was inevitable is immaterial to us now. What is important is that we should recognize that, from the very beginning of the Christian era, human fear and profane arrogance, far more than the teachings of Jesus, dictated the course of Chris-tianity. An elaborate man-made system, derived as much from Jewish and Greek philosophical systems as from the teachings of Jesus, evolved as a powerful instrument in the hands of men at least as interested in power and domination as they were in taking up their cross and following the path of their founder.

The Edict of Milan (AD 313) still paid lip-service to tolerance of religious beliefs and ways of worship, but soon the State betrayed a heavy bias in favor of Christianity, and in less than fifty years other religions were being persecuted in the name of Jesus. Not only this, but also an enforced uniformity, to be verbally expressed in the form of a creed, was demanded of all who called themselves Christians; 'heretics' were pursued with as much bitterness and violence as were pagans. It is interesting to note here that Christianity was never called a religion until after the Constantinian settlement, thus underlining Guénon's contention that 'religions' are to be placed at a lower level than Religion, the true light that lighteth every man that cometh into the world.

On the accession of Theodosius in AD 379 the policy of the suppression of all opinions contrary to those deemed by the authorities to be orthodox was given full rein. The Church set about what it believed to be its divinely appointed task—the extirpation of paganism and the ruthless suppression of all heretics:

> The Church ceased to be a voluntary private organization comparable to other social organizations and became instead a compulsory, all-inclusive and coercive society comparable to what we call 'the state' and in its totality well nigh indistinguishable from it.[1]

Or as another Church historian has said

> We can conceive no greater gulf between two ideas or principles than that which separates the disciple of the first century, gladly

---

1. F. Oakley, *The Crucial Centuries* (1979), p 53.

taking up his Cross to follow Christ, from the terrorized proselyte of the fifth or sixth century accepting baptism as the alternative to banishment and the loss of all that he possessed.[2]

Even the greatest figures of the time, such as Ambrose and Augustine, believed in persecution as a legitimate means of extending Christ's Kingdom. The legacy of such attitudes remains with us even today. Our dependence on force as a means of imposing on others what we believe to be true, our presumption that Church and State should be allies, and our reluctance to reject earthly power as a means of achieving spiritual aims are all in direct contradiction to the universal Primordial Tradition. All these errors are essentially errors of emphasis typical of the West, an emphasis on the external, a reluctance to seek first the Kingdom of Heaven which is within us. But Providence, in these last days, has given us the means of redressing this imbalance.

Various factors, which previously did not exist, have in recent years made possible better understanding and more ready acceptance of points of view which were formerly incomprehensible or simply unknown—in particular, the remarkable penetration of the Western world by Eastern ideas.

Much, however, of what passes for Eastern thought is spurious and is aimed at exploiting Western ignorance and credulity for financial gain and personal power. But there is also genuine teaching of great value. The exodus of Buddhist monks from Tibet to the West has enabled many to have direct contact with authentic teaching and has given a great spur to the translation of sacred texts. The same may be said of the Vedanta movement and certain Islamic teachings. The *Tao Te Ching* and certain Zen Classics have been well translated and are widely read and sometimes even taught by well qualified teachers free of Western bias.

In France in particular Guénon himself and his writings have provided a focus for a small but influential group of scholars who are exploring the ramifications of the Primordial Tradition as expounded by Guénon.

---

2. W. Hobhouse, *The Church and the World in Idea and History* (1910), p108.

In the more specifically Christian sphere the work of Emile Gillabert and the Centre de Recherche Métaphysique de Marsanne is of importance. Gillabert's work is centered on the recently discovered Gospel of Thomas as a means of discovering those elements of Jesus' teaching that were omitted by the compilers of the canonical gospels. In his book *Paroles de Jésus et Pensée Orientale* he makes a strong case for saying that, in its essence, the teaching of Jesus is closely allied to the traditional teaching of the East:

> So in the end the true teaching of Jesus freed from its national and apocalyptic context and cleansed from the coloring of the epoch and place of origin and compared with the great teachings of the East such as the Vedas, the Upanishads, the Bhagavad-Gita, the Tao, the Tch'an, is revealed to us in its universal aspect. With this perspective the only possible in a world where modern science stands in opposition to anthropomorphic and anthropocentric religions, the Judeo-Christian phenomenon is reduced to an epiphenomenon of civilization, destined to disappear in the devastating flood which it itself has engendered while the original message of Jesus, always contemporary because it is beyond time, is found to be capable of satisfying the exigencies of the savant as well as answering the questions of the metaphysician.[3]

Some may consider that this wholesale condemnation of the man-centeredness of the Judeo-Christian tradition is unbalanced. But Gillabert's devotion to the Rabbi of Nazareth and his teaching, as well as his scholarship, are impressive and his ideas deserve careful and open-minded consideration.

In his *Apologia pro Vita Sua* Cardinal Newman wrote:

> Nothing can be presented to me, in time to come, as part of the faith, but what I ought already to have received, and hitherto have been kept from receiving, (if so) merely because it has not been brought home to me. Nothing can be imposed on me different in kind from what I hold already—much less contrary to it. The new truth which is promulgated, if it is to be called new,

---

3. E. Gillabert, loc. cit., p9.

must be at least homogeneous, cognate, implicit, viewed relatively, to the old truth. It must be what I may even have guessed, or wished to be included. . . . Perhaps I and others have always actually believed it. . . .[4]

We do not need to be defensive in our attitude to the new, for that is to deny the possibility of change under the guidance of the Holy Spirit, and we can surely say with Gamaliel, 'If this counsel or this work be of men, it will come to naught. But if it be of God ye cannot overthrow it; lest haply ye be found even to fight against God' (Acts 5:38–9).

So be it! Maranatha!

---

4. J. H. Newman, *Apologia pro Vita Sua* (Oxford, World's Classics edn.), p 263.

SELECT BIBLIOGRAPHY

A COMPREHENSIVE BIBLIOGRAPHY of Guénon has been published in Canada by Laval University Press. The list below contains only the main items and those works used by the author. Unless otherwise indicated, all current works in English are published by Sophia Perennis in Hillsdale, NY. All works in French are published in Paris. Only original dates of publication in France are given, although most titles have been reprinted several times.

PART ONE

WORKS BY RENÉ GUÉNON

Introduction Générale à l'Étude des Doctrines Hindoues (1921).
Le Théosophisme: Histoire d'une Pseudo-Religion (1921); second, revised edn., 1925.
L'Erreur Spirite (1923).
Orient et Occident (1924).
L'Homme et son Devenir selon le Vedānta (1925).
L'Ésotérisme de Dante (1925).
Le Roi du Monde (1927).
La Crise du Monde Moderne (1927).
Autorité Spirituelle et Pouvoir Temporel (1929).
St Bernard (1929); pamphlet.
Le Symbolisme de la Croix (1931).
Les États Multiples de l'Être (1932).
La Métaphysique Orientale (1939); his only public lecture.
Le Règne de la Quantité et les Signes des Temps (1945); his *magnum opus*.

Les Principes du Calcul Infinitésimal (1946).
Aperçus sur l'Initiation (1946); reworked from published articles.
La Grande Triad (1946).

WORKS PUBLISHED AFTER GUÉNON'S DEATH

Most of these works consist of reprints of Guénon's contributions to periodicals, arranged according to subject.

Initiation et Réalisation Spirituelle (1952).
Aperçus sur l'Ésotérisme chrétien (1954).
Symboles de la Science Sacrée (1962).
Études sur la Franc-Maçonnerie et le Compagnonnage (1973), two volumes.
Études sur l'Hindouisme (1968).
Formes Traditionnelles et Cycles Cosmiques (1970).
Aperçus sur l'Ésotérisme Islamique et le Taoïsme (1973).
Comptes rendus (1973).
Mélanges (1976).

THE FOLLOWING TRANSLATIONS OF GUÉNON'S WORKS HAVE APPEARED IN ENGLISH.

The Crisis of the Modern World (1942, 1962, 1975, 1996, 2001).
East and West (1941, 1995, 2001).
The Esoterism of Dante (1996, 2001).
The Great Triad (1991, 2001).
Initiation and the Crafts (Ipswich, 1973). Pamphlet
Initiation and Spiritual Realization (2001).
Insights into Christian Esoterism (2001). Contains translation of the pamphlet *St Bernard*.
Introduction to the Study of the Hindu Doctrines (1945, 2001).
The King of the World (1983 [as *The Lord of the World*], 2001).
Man and His Becoming according to the Vedānta (1928, 1945, 2001).

The Multiple States of the Being (1984, 2001).
Perspectives on Initiation (2001).
The Reign of Quantity and the Signs of the Times (1953, 1972, 1995, 2001).
Spiritual Authority and Temporal Power (2001).
Studies in Hinduism (partial translation, 1985, New Delhi; new and complete translation, 2001). Contains translation of *La Métaphysique Orientale.*
Symbolism of the Cross (1958, 1975, 1996, 2001).

ENGLISH TRANSLATIONS IN PRESS OR
SCHEDULED FOR PUBLICATION 2003–2004:

Insights into Islamic Esoterism and Taoism.
The Metaphysical Principles of the Infinitesimal Calculus.
Miscellanea.
The Spiritist Fallacy.
Studies in Freemasonry and the Compagnonnage.
Symbols of Sacred Science (first edition, as *Fundamental Symbols: The Universal Language of Sacred Science*, 1995).
Theosophy: History of a Pseudo-Religion.
Traditional Forms and Cosmic Cycles.

PART TWO

WORKS ABOUT GUÉNON

Abd al Wahed, *In Memoriam René Guénon* (Milano, 1981); a short perceptive obituary.

Andruzac, C., *René Guénon, La contemplation métaphysique et l'expérience mystique* (1980). Has the official imprimatur and is a rather pedestrian analysis, which somehow misses the point.

Batache, Eddy, *Surréalisme et Tradition* (1978). A most interesting approach to Guénon and the Surrealists.

Chacornac, Paul, *La Vie Simple de René Guénon* (1958; new edition 1982). An essential biographical document by an old friend. English translation, *The Simple Life of René Guénon*, scheduled for publication in 2003.

Chaleil, André, *Les Grands Initiés de Notre Temps* (1978); pp 115–143 are devoted to Guénon—uninspired.

Colloque international de Cerisy-la-Salle, July 13–20, 1973, *René Guénon et l'Actualité de la Pensée Traditionnelle*. Actes du Colloque... (Milano, 1980). An essential work.

Cologne, Daniel, *Julius Evola, René Guénon et le Christianisme* (1978). A most interesting comparison of these two very different figures.

Coomaraswamy, A. K., *The Bugbear of Literacy* (1949, 1979). Chap. 4 (pp 64–77) is devoted to a study of Guénon; wise and sympathetic, by a friend and admirer.

Daniélou, J., *Essai sur le mystère de l'Histoire* (1953); pp 120–6 contain an article 'Grandeur et faiblesse de René Guénon'. This work has also appeared in English.

Études Traditionnelles Numéro Spécial consacré a René Guénon (1951; facsimile reprint, 1982). A most valuable series of articles by friends and admirers with a list of translations of Guénon's works into European languages.

James, Marie-France, *Ésotérisme et Christianisme autour de René Guénon* (*Ésotérisme, Occultisme, Franc-Maçonnerie, et Christianisme aux XIXe et XXe siècles. Explorations bio-bibliographiques*), two volumes (1981). A pioneer work, inevitably inaccurate in some details and more seriously marred by the author's confused and somewhat biased approach.

Laurent, J. P., *Le Sens caché dans l'Oeuvre de René Guénon* (Lausanne, 1975). A most valuable work, with much original biographical information.

Marcineau, J., *René Guénon et son Oeuvre* (Poitiers, 1946).

Meroz, L., *René Guénon ou la Sagesse Initiatique* (1962). Of no great value.

Ravignant, P., *Les Maîtres Spirituel Contemporains* (1972); pp 130–135 are on Guénon but are of little value.

Reghini, A., *Les Nombres Sacrés dans la Tradition Pythagoricienne*

Maçonnique (Milano, 1981). Includes ten letters from Guénon.

Robin, J., *René Guénon. Témoin de la Tradition* (1978) and *René Guénon: La Dernière Chance de L'Occident* (1983). Robin's books are primarily concerned with 'ce grand guénonien que fut le Général de Gaulle' and only marginally of interest for Guénon himself.

Roman, Denys (pseud., Marcel Mangy), *René Guénon et les Destins de la Franc-Maçonnerie* (1982). A sympathetic account of Guénon's importance for Freemasonry.

Sérant, P., *René Guénon. 2ᵉ édition revue et augmentée* (1977). A serious work, but marred by the author's religious bias.

Sigaud, P.M. (ed.), *René Guénon. Dossier H* (Lausanne, 1984). Contains many valuable contributions and a useful bibliography.

Tourniac, Jean, *Propos sur René Guénon* (1973). Valuable.

Valsan, M., *L'Islam et la Fonction de René Guénon* (1984). A posthumous collection of valuable articles.

PART THREE

WORKS CONSULTED AND OF
INTEREST TO STUDENTS OF GUÉNON.

d'Alveydre, Saint Yves, *Clefs de l'Orient*, édition intégrale (Nice, 1980). A work much used by Guénon.

Baylot, Jean, *Oswald Wirth 1860–1943, Renovateur et Mainteneur de la Véritable Franc-Maçonnerie* (1975). References to Guénon, of whom Wirth did not really approve.

Benoist, Luc., *La Cuisine des Anges, un essai sur la formation du langage. Littérature et Tradition* (Rennes, 1978). The second essay appeared in English as *Literature and Tradition* in 1969.

—*L'Art du Monde. La spiritualité du Métier* (1978). Much influenced by Guénon.

—*L'Ésotérisme*, 5th edn., (1980). The best general work, giving an excellent background for the understanding of Guénon's writings. English translation, *The Esoteric Path: An Introduction to the Hermetic Tradition* (1988, 2003).

Borella, J., *La Charité profanée* (1979). A profound theological work much influenced by Guénon and Eastern philosophy. Also *Ésotérisme guénonien et mystère chrétien* (1997).

Chenique, F., *Le Buisson ardent* (1972). By a Christian student of Guénon and of considerable interest.

Corneloup, J., *Je ne sais qu'épeler* (Paris, 1971). Chapter four.

Eliade, M., *Occultism, Witchcraft, and Cultural Fashions. Essays in Comparative Religions* (University of Chicago Press, 1976). Interesting references to Guénon. Eliade's many books in English and French are a valuable adjunct to Guénon's works.

Encausse, P., *Papus: le Balzac de l'Occultisme* (1979). The standard life by his son.

Faucher, J.A., *Histoire de la Grande Loge de France 1738–1980*. Includes an account of the Grande Triade Lodge.

Georgel, Gaston, *L'Ère Future et le Mouvement de l'Histoire* (1956). Georgel is one of the very few balanced writers on this subject. He received help and encouragement from Guénon.

—*Les Quatres Âges de l'Humanité*, second edition (Milano, 1976). Dedicated to Guénon and with an introductory letter from him.

—*Les Rhythmes dans l'Histoire*, third edition (Milano, 1981).

—*Le Cycle Judeo-Chrétien* (Milano, 1983).

Gillabert, E., *Saint Paul ou la Colosse aux Pieds d'Argile* (1974).

—*Jésus et la Gnose* (1981).

—*Paroles de Jésus et Pensée Orientale* (Marsanne, 1984). Many appreciative references to Guénon.

Hani, Jean, *La Divine Liturgie* (1981).

—*Les Métiers de Dieu. Préliminaires à une spiritualité du travail* (1975).

—*Le Symbolisme du Temple Chrétien* (1962). Hani's books, though thoroughly orthodox, are very conscious of and sympathetic to Guénon.

Lao Tzu, *Tao Te Ching*. A new translation by Gia-Fu Feng and Jane English (1974). The best English translation.

Laurant, J.P., *Matgioi, un aventurier taoïste* (Paris, 1982). The only biography of Guénon's teacher in Taoism.

Marsaudon, Y., *De l'Initiation maçonnique à l'Orthodoxie chrétienne* (Paris, 1965).

Michelet, V.-E., *Les Compagnons de la Hiérophanie* (n.d.). Reminiscences of the Hermetic movement at the end of the nineteenth century.

Moine d'Orient, un, *Doctrine de la Non-Dualité (advaita-vada) et Christianisme* (Paris, 1982). Takes note of Guénon's work.

Schaya, Léo, *The Universal Meaning of the Kabbalah* (1971). Guénonian in outlook.

Schuon, Frithjof, *Christianity/Islam: Essays in Esoteric Ecumenicism* (1985).

—*Light on the Ancient Worlds* (1966). Schuon has written many other books. He was at one time very close to Guénon, but they eventually parted company. Most of his books have been translated into English.

Servier, J., *L'Homme et l'Invisible* (1980). Although not explicitly Guénonian, the author, an ethnologist, lends support to many of Guénon's views.

Stéphane, L'Abbé Henri, *Introduction à l'Ésotérisme Chrétien. Traités Recueillis par François Chenique*. Preface by Jean Borella (Paris, 1979–83). Two volumes by a Christian priest who admired and understood Guénon, but not uncritically.

Studies in Comparative Religion. A.K. Coomaraswamy Centenary Issue (Summer 1977). Contains much of interest to students of Guénon, as do the three volumes of Coomaraswamy's *Collected Papers,* published by the Bollingen Foundation.

Tourniac, J., *Lumière d'Orient des Chrétientés d'Asie aux Mystérés évangéliques* (Paris, 1979). Much influenced by Guénon.

—*Symbolisme Maçonnique et Tradition Chrétienne* (1965; reprint 1982).

—*Melkitsedeq ou la Tradition Primordiale* (1983). Entirely Guénonian in tone.

Vallin, G., *La Perspective Métaphysique* (1977). The results of twenty years' study, in an academic context, of Guénon's work. Very valuable.

Vulliaud, P., *La Kabbale juive* (1923; reprinted 1976). The standard work much used by Guénon.

INDEX

Advaita Vedanta 51, 58–63, 80, 108, 116
Agarttha 31, 40
Aguéli, Ivan Gustaf 28–31
Alchemy 21, 82, 110
Anizan, Fr Felix 41
Apollonius of Tyana 21
Aristotle 57
Arjuna 63
Augustine, St 89, 102, 118, 129, 137

Bammate, Nadjmoud-Dine 4, 46, 79
Barfield, Owen 104 n 4, 108 n 6
Batache, Eddy 6
Belile, Françoise 35, 42
Berdyaev, Nicolas 91–94, 98–100
Bergson, Henri 19–20
Blake, William 2
Blavatsky, H. P. 23, 30, 71
Blois 11–12, 16, 18, 35, 47
Bosco, Henri 54
Bossard Abbé 13–14
Bricaud, Jean 24
Buddhism 28, 47
Burroughs, William 3

Caste system 75–76, 79, 84, 122
Chacornac, Paul 19, 34, 38–39, 43–44, 62
Champrenaud, Léon 23–24, 28–29
Chamuel, Lucien 23

Charbonneau-Lassay 41, 45
China 40, 79
Church Catholic 25, 34, 40, 51, 112, 133, Gnostic 23
Clarin de la Rive 32–34
Clavelle, Maurice 45
Clement of Alexandria 52, 102–103, 126
Coleridge, Samuel T. 18, 58, 83, 104, 108, 112
Collège Augustin-Thierry 14–15, 19, 35
Collège Rollin 16, 21
Compagnonnage 115
Comte, Auguste 19
Coomaraswamy, A. K. 47, 55
Corbin, Henri 130
Corbusier 3

D'Alveydre, Alexandra St Yves 31
Davancourt, Simon 31
De Chardin, Teilhard 113
De Frémond, Olivier 45
De Gaulle, General 20
De Molay, Jacques 2, 51
De Sarachaga, Baron Alexis 41
Detré, Charles 25
Deutsch, Eliot 61
Dina, Madame 30, 43
Dionysius the Areopagite 28, 58, 61, 64, 81
Dodd, C. H. 127
Doinel, Jules 23
Duru, Madame 12, 17, 31, 35, 42

Eckhart, Meister 61, 81, 83, 93, 112
Eliade, Mircea 50–51, 90–91, 96
Eliot, T.S. 20, 61
Elish El-Kabir, Shaykh Abder Rahmen 29, 74
Elite 31, 62, 75–76, 85, 93, 130
Encausse, Gérard (see Papus) 21

Fabre des Essarts, Léonce 23-24
Fourier 31
Freemasonry 19, 21, 24, 32, 51, 115, 122, 124
Freud, Sigmund 51, 109
Fuller, Buckminster 67
Fyodorov, N.F. 88

Gandhi 76, 122
Gasset, Ortega y 3
Germain, Pierre 36
Ghyka, Matila 131
Gide, André 54
Gillabert, Emile 138
Gnose, La 26, 29–30, 34
Golden Dawn, Hermetic Order of 26
Gombault, Abbé Ferdinand 17–18
Great Triad 18, 46, 62, 92, 124
Grangier, Dr Tony 39, 43
Grousset, René 40
Guaita, Stanislas 22
Guenon, Berthe 35, 39, 42–43
Günther, H. 76
Gurdjieff 71

Hani, Jean 6
Harrison, J.F.C. 97–98
Haven, Marc 22
Hermetic Brotherhood of Luxor, 72
Hippolitus of Rome 52

Howe, Ellic 25
Huot, Marie 28

Ibn Arabi 29, 73, 76
Ile St Louis 16, 38, 44
Incantation 119
Irenaeus, St 82

James, Marie-France 34, 39
Jogand, Gabriel 33
Joyce, James 3
Jung, C.G. 86–87, 92, 132

Kabbalah 21, 31, 81–82, 101, 104
Kadmon, Adam 81–82, 103
Kali-Yuga 76, 96
Kardec, Allan 23
Knights Templar 2, 42, 51, 122

Lao Tzu 24
Laurant, J.P. 16
Leclère, Albert 15–16, 19
Lelande, Emmanuel 22
Le Loup, Yvon (see Paul Sédir), 22, 30
Lesueur, Dr 35
Lévi, Sylvain 36
Lévi, Eliphas 18
Levy, John 44
Logos 29, 52, 81
Loury, Berthe 17
Luther 2

Manu 95–96, 128
Manvantara 2, 96–97
Maritain, Jacques 36, 40, 58, 71
Marx, Karl 51
Matgioi 23–24, 30, 70
Maurice-Denis, Noële 36
Mcluhan, Marshal 67
Melchizedek 125–130

Ménard, François 62
Merton, Thomas 1, 89–90
Métraux, Alfred 68
Meunier, Mario 43
Michelet, Victor-Emil 21
Milarepa 7
Morris, William 26

Neo-thomism 36
Neumann, Erich 109
Newman, John Henry 111, 138–139
Nostalgia 41, 87–88

Oedipus, complex 109
Orain, Canon 12
Order of the Temple 23
Ordo Templum Orientis 26
Ossendowski, Ferdinand 40, 42

Palingenius (pseudonym of René Guénon)) 24
Palladism 33
Pallis, Marco 47
Papus (see Gérard Encausse) 25, 28, 31
Pascal 90
Peilleaube, Emile 36
Peladan 22
Pernety, Dom 123
Pestalozzi 22
Philippe, Maître 22
Picasso, Pablo 3
Plato 102
Pouvourville, Albert de (see Matgioi) 23–24, 28–29
Prajapati 95
Pralaya 96
Pythagoras 102

Rahner, Hugo 53

Rahner, Karl 94
Ramanuja 60
Rasputin 22
Regnabit 41
Reincarnation 72
Renaissance 2
Reuss, Theodore 25–26
Reyor, Jean 45
Rivail, Hippolyte 22
Rose-Croix 22, 30–31
Rosicrucians 21, 30, 51, 122
Rosnay, Baron de 41
Rougier, Louis 56–57
Ruysbroeck 58

Sacred Heart of Jesus 20, 41
Sacred Numbers 130
Saivism 96
Salama Radi, Shaykh 44
Sartre, Jean-Paul 3
Saunier, Jean 31
Schuon, Frithjof 47
Schmemann 88
Scholem G. 104
Sédir, Paul (see Yvon le Loup), 22, 30–31
Servier, Jean 68–69, 116
Seth 127
Setif 35
Shakespeare 70
Shankara 60
Shiva 51
Sigaud, Pierre-Marie 6, 54
Spiritualist Movement 22, 26, 72
Spiritualist-Masonic Congress, 23–24
Stéphane, Henri 6
Sufism 28–30, 43, 118
Surrealism 3, 6
Swedenborg 26, 28, 123
Synarchie 31

Tagore, Rabindranath 70
Tarot 21–22
Taxil, Leo 33–35
Taylor, Bishop John 107
Teder 25
Teilhard 113
Temple, Archbishop William, 78-80
Teresa, Mother 70
Theosophy 27–23, 26–30, 38, 71–72, 123
Theodosius 136
Tourniac, Jean 128–129
Truc, Gonzague 39–40, 42

Valsan, Michel 73–74
Varro 117
Vaughan, Diana 33–34
Vedanta 18, 20, 30–31, 51, 59–65, 70, 80–82, 90, 96, 137
Vishnu 77
Vivekananda, Swami 30
Vreede, Frans 39
Vuilliaud, Paul 102

Wu-wu-wei 70, 103

Yarker, John 25–26

Zen 137

Printed in France by Amazon
Brétigny-sur-Orge, FR